AF394481

FACING
Our Fears,
RELEASING
Our Faith
Workbook

FACING *Our Fears,* RELEASING *Our Faith*

Workbook

Kingdom of Satan, Kingdom of God

Deborah A. Ward

XULON PRESS

Xulon Press
2301 Lucien Way #415
Maitland, FL 32751
407.339.4217
www.xulonpress.com

© 2020 by Deborah A. Ward

All rights reserved solely by the author. The author guarantees all contents are original and do not infringe upon the legal rights of any other person or work. No part of this book may be reproduced in any form without the permission of the author. The views expressed in this book are not necessarily those of the publisher.

Unless otherwise indicated, Scripture quotations taken from the King James Version (KJV)–*public domain*.

Printed in the United States of America

Paperback ISBN-13: 978-1-6322-1341-9
Ebook ISBN-13: 978-1-6322-1342-6

PREFACE

*F*acing Our Fears, Releasing Our Faith by Deborah A. Ward is the workbook companion to the author's book of the same name. In the pages of the workbook, reader's will learn how to stand up against the enemy. Satan has set up a highly systemized army, with rank and order, to energize the ungodly and to attack the believers. "The thief cometh not, but to steal, and to kill, and to destroy, (John 10:10a)."

God has set up a higher systemized army of believers to combat the plan of the enemy. The key is to renew the mind to the things of God.

> "Jesus came that they may have life, and have it more abundantly,
> (John 10:10b)."

The intent of this workbook is to first reveal the enemy and his wiles. Secondly, to reveal the truth of God's Word that will make one totally free.

> "And ye shall know the truth, and the truth shall make you free,
> (John 8:32)."

CONTENTS

The Two Kingdoms:

" THE KINGDOM OF LIGHT &
THE KINGDOM OF DARKNESS"

The world we live in is composed of two Kingdoms. There is the "Kingdom of Light or the Kingdom of God" (God being the Creator). This Kingdom is a theocracy (system of government ruled by God). He is the King of Kings, and Lord of Lords. He created the world and everything in it, the Heaven and Earth, animals, firmament, people; everything. He rules through His Son Jesus. God's Kingdom operates by <u>FAITH,</u> which is a system of belief.

The other Kingdom is the "Kingdom of Darkness or Kingdom of Satan" (Satan). This Kingdom is ruled by Satan who is the <u>god</u> of this world, the prince of the power of the air, the devil. He is assisted by principalities, powers, rulers of darkness and spiritual wickedness in high places. These powers of darkness are spiritual rulers of the world who energize the ungodly, oppose God's will, and frequently attack the believers of this age. They constitute a vast multitude and are organized into a highly systemized empire of evil spirits with rank and order. Satan's Kingdom operates by <u>FEAR.</u>

We must know that Satan is the arch enemy of God. He does everything in his power to keep us from inheriting the Kingdom of God, to steal our faith in God, to kill our testimony for Christ, and to take us into eternal damnation. He is a thief who came to steal, kill, and destroy (John 10:10) everything that God has created. We must also know that Jesus came so that He would give us the life of Christ. That life which is lived on a much higher plain, abundantly, richly, and to the full, eternal life. It is God's intent through His Word to reveal the wiles of the devil to us. Secondly, to reveal the truth of His Word that will make us totally free, as we understand and receive it.

Wile is defined as a trick, artifice or strategy meant to fool, trap, deceive or entice; slyness, craftiness. Satan does all of this to us before we come to know Jesus. He deceives us into believing that we are missing out on all the good or the fun things of life. He entices us into the very things that will destroy us, and we fall into his web of deceit because of the FEAR of not ever being able to "do or have certain things." He lures us into counterfeit relationships as a substitute for real (agape) love. He causes us to desire things out of season, which plunge everything out of order.

Satan has perverted, or turned away from the right course of action, everything that God made. Until we come to the realization of what he has done, we will not be able to distinguish what is right from what is wrong. He has confused the mind of man.

Because of the disobedience of Adam and Eve, every person born into this world is born with a sinful nature. This is done under Satan's authority. Because we were born with a sinful nature, it is hard to distinguish the light from the darkness. Darkness comes automatically, but our minds have to be renewed to the things of God (light). We must change our way of thinking, or renew our minds to the mind of Christ, or we will remain in a state of confusion. We must accept Jesus as our Savior, and be transformed by the renewing of our minds (Rom. 12:2). The way to renew our mind is through the Word of God, (The Bible).

THE TWO KINGDOMS REVIEW:

1. The world we live in is composed of two Kingdoms. Name them.

____

____

2. The Kingdom of Light is ruled by _________________________.

3. The Kingdom of Darkness is ruled by _____________________.

4. Who created the world and everything in it?

____

5. God rules through His Son _______________________________.

6. The Kingdom of God is what type of government?

____

7. The Kingdom of God operates by _________________________.

8. Faith is a system_____________________________________.

9. In the Kingdom of Darkness, Satan is assisted by ___________________

____

____

____

10. Satan is in an agreement with God. True or False?

11. Satan's Kingdom is motivated or operates by

____

12. Is Satan a friend or an enemy of God? _______________________

13. After the fall of Adam and Eve, every person that is born into this world is born with a ____.

14. Satan is a thief. True or False? (Circle the answer)

15. In order to leave the Kingdom of Darkness we must be

____

16. After we are born again it is important to

____

____

17. Why is it important to change your way of thinking? Explain:____

____

____

18. How do you renew your mind?

____

THE KINGDOM OF DARKNESS-"SATAN'S KINGDOM" (FACING OUR FEARS)

After the fall of Adam and Eve, every person born comes into this world with a sinful (selfish) nature. We will begin our study with the "Kingdom of Darkness." This corruption of human nature involves the inborn desire to go our own selfish way, without concern for God or others, which is passed on to ALL human beings.

In the "Kingdom of Darkness," the Devil, our adversary, is totally opposed to the "Kingdom of Light" or the "Kingdom of God. He is totally evil. He can do no right. There is no good in him. He is evil, which means "morally wrong; immoral, wicked, injurious, destructive, unrighteous, disastrous." Satan is a thief who comes to steal, kill and destroy (John 10:10). He is the Father of Lies. He is a murderer and a sower of discord. He is opposed to everything that God says. He is cunning. He is a coward. He is without principles. He is proud and deceitful. He is fierce, cruel, and aggressive.

The term "devil" reflects both Satan's character, and the strategy he uses against human beings. Concerning his character, there is no truth in him. Concerning his strategy, the devil used lies to draw Eve into sin (Genesis 3:1-5), and he twisted the truth when tempting Jesus (Matthew 4:6). He is so opposed to Jesus that everything God has done has been perverted by the enemy or adversary.

Satan has set up a highly systemized army, or empire of evil spirit forces, with rank and order. They rule this world. He uses his forces to lure us from loyalty to Christ, and into the sins of the world. He wants to entice us into the works of the flesh. Believers are to instruct those who reject and oppose Christianity, "In the hope that God will grant them repentance leading them to the knowledge of the truth, and that they will come to their senses and escape from the trap of the devil, who has taken them captive to do his will," (2 Timothy 2:25,26).

Although the believer is in spiritual warfare with Satan (the battle the Christian fights to overcome the strategies and snares of the forces of darkness) on a daily basis, Christ has obtained the victory through His death on the cross. He waged a triumphant battle against Satan, disarmed the evil powers and authorities of wickedness, set captives free, and redeemed the believer from Satan's dominion (Acts 26:18).

THE WORKS OF THE FLESH

The flesh is the sinful element in human nature, with its corrupt desires. The flesh is a mindset, a way of thinking (the world's way of thinking). The world's way of thinking means everything that is opposed to God, His Kingdom, and His righteousness.

"Now the works of the flesh are manifest, which are these; Adultery, fornication, lasciviousness, idolatry, witchcraft, hatred, variance, emulation, wrath, strife, sedition, heresy, envying, murder, drunkenness, reveling, and such like: of the which I tell you before, as I have also told you in time past, that they which do such things shall not inherit the Kingdom of God" (Galatians 5:19-21).

The Bible lists a few of the sins of the flesh, but there are actually about 613 of these laws (sins). God does not want us to be conformed to the ways of the world, or the ways of Satan, but He wants us to be transformed by the renewing of our minds through the Word of God (Romans 12:2). Even after we are born-again, it is of utmost importance that we renew our minds so we can change our way of thinking. If our minds are not renewed to the things of God, we will continue in our old way of thinking. The sinful nature remains in us and is a deadly enemy to us. "Study and be eager and do your utmost to present yourself to God approved (tested by trial), a workman who has no cause to be ashamed, correctly analyzing and accurately dividing, rightly handling and skillfully teaching the word of truth," (2 Timothy 2:15 Amp).

THE KINGDOM OF DARKNESS: (SATAN'S KINGDOM) REVIEW:

1. **With the fall of Adam and Eve, what nature was passed on to all humans?**

____

2. **Who is our adversary (the born-again Christian)?** ___________________

____

3. **Name 4 characteristics of Satan:**

____

____

____

____

4. **Satan has perverted (corrupted or distorted) everything God made.**

True   False

5. **What type of army does Satan have?** _________________________

____

6. **Even though Satan is in a constant battle with us, we have the victory. How?**

____

7. The believer has been ____

    from Satan's dominion.

8. What is the flesh? ____

    ____

9. Name 4 works of the flesh according to (Galatians 5:19-21).

    ____

    ____

    ____

10. The Bible list only a few works of the flesh, but there are

    ____in all.

DESCRIPTION OF THE WORKS OF THE FLESH

FORNICATION

The first description of the flesh we will look at is fornication. The Random House Dictionary describes fornication as voluntary, sexual intercourse between two unmarried persons. It is immoral sexual conduct and intercourse. It is having sex outside of the bonds of marriage.

Fornication is the one sin that most Christians are not willing to give up, because of the sexual and physical pleasure that comes with it. They feel that their sexual desire is too strong to give up this sexual sin for the Lord. Even though the temptation to fornicate is put before us almost every day of our life in some form or fashion. We must not underestimate the power of it. This sin has devastated countless lives, destroyed families, churches, communities, and even nations.

We watch movies and television where sex outside of marriage is looked at as a normal behavior, even desirable. Meanwhile, marriage is considered to be borin or confining or even joyless. If we keep ourselves pure until marriage, we are looked down on by others. Why is this? Let me tell you why, the mind needs to be renewed. Until we fully understand God's Word, we are subject to the entrapment of the enemy. We allow our own selfish desires to outweigh obedience. We feel like, "Oh, God will understand. I think He will cut me some slack in this area because He knows how hard it is." Even though God loves us, He cannot change or be separated from His Word.

Scriptures in the Bible concerning fornication:

"Now the body is not for fornication, but for the Lord; and the Lord
   for the body," (1 Corinthians 6:13).

"Know ye not that your bodies are the members of Christ? Shall I then take the members of Christ, and make them the members of a harlot? God forbid. What? Know ye not that he which is joined to a harlot is one body? For two, saith he, shall be one flesh. But he that is joined unto the Lord is one Spirit. Flee fornication. Every sin that a man doeth is without the body; but he that committeth fornication sinneth against his own body. What? Know ye not that your body is the temple of the Holy Ghost which is in you. Which ye have of God, and ye are not your own? For you were bought with a price; therefore glorify God in your body and in your spirit, which are God's, (1 Corinthians 6:15-20)."

When a believer joins his/her body to an immoral person he/she becomes one with that person, to come under his/her domination (Genesis 2:24), to desecrate what the cross has made holy, and to sever himself from the Kingdom of God.

Your body as a Christian is the personal dwelling place of the Holy Spirit. The Holy Spirit is God's mark on you that you belong to Him, (Romans 8:11). Because He dwells in you and you belong to God, your body must never be defiled by any impurity or evil, whether by immoral thoughts, desires, deeds, films, books, or magazines.

You must live in such a way as to glorify and please God in your body.

"Be ye therefore followers of God, as dear children; and walk in love,
   as Christ also hath loved us, and hath given himself for us an offering
   and a sacrifice to God for a sweet-smelling savour. But fornication and
   all uncleanness, or covetousness, let it not be once named among you,
   as becometh saints; neither filthiness, nor foolish talking, nor jesting,
   which are not convenient; but rather giving thanks," (Ephesians 5:1-4).

Just as children imitate their parents, we should imitate Christ. His great love for us led him to sacrifice Himself, so that we could live. We should love others the same way, with a love that goes beyond affection to self-sacrificing service.

We should consider ourselves dead and unresponsive to sexual immorality, impurity, lust, evil desires, and greed. Just like diseased limbs on a tree, these practices should be cut off before they destroy us. We must make a conscious daily decision to remove anything and everything that supports or feeds these desires, and to rely on the Holy Spirit's power.

The temptation to engage in sexual intercourse outside of the marriage relationship has always been powerful. Giving in to that temptation can have disastrous results. Sexual sins always hurt someone, either physically or spiritually. Sexual desires and activities must be placed under Christ's control. God created sex for procreation and pleasure, and is an expression of love between a husband and wife. Sexual experience must be limited to the marriage relationship to avoid hurting ourselves, our relationship with God, and our relationships with others.

> "Do you not know that the wicked will not inherit the Kingdom of God? Do not be deceived: Neither the sexually immoral, nor idolaters, nor adulterers, nor male prostitutes, nor homosexual offenders, nor thieves, nor the greedy, nor drunkards, nor slanderers, nor swindlers, will inherit the Kingdom of God. And you were sanctified, you were justified in the name of the Lord Jesus Christ and by the Spirit of God," (1 Corinthians 6:9-11).

Here Paul is describing the characteristics of unbelievers. He doesn't mean that idolaters, adulterers, male prostitutes, homosexuals, thieves, greedy-people, drunkards, slanderers or swindlers are automatically and irrevocably excluded from Heaven. Christians come out of all kinds of different backgrounds, including these. They may still struggle with evil desires, but try not to continue in the same practice. Paul clearly states that even those who sin in these ways can have their lives changed by Christ.

Although fornication is popular in our culture, we as Christians do not have to take part in it. We are free to be all that we can be for God, but we are not free from God. God created sex to be a beautiful and essential ingredient of marriage, but sex outside of the relationship will always hurt someone.

Prepare for the attractive temptations that will come your way. Of course, we cannot always prevent temptation, but there is a way of escape (1 Corinthians 10:13). Allow God's Word and God's people to help you to stand against sin. Whenever we leave God out of our plans, we are placing ourselves above Him. This is exactly what Satan wants us to do. Sin is always striving to gain control over us.

Believers should not be in voluntary partnership or in intimate relationships with unbelievers. Even if a friend is professing to be a Christian, and cannot see eye to eye with what you believe, get away from that person. This type of relationship will corrupt your relationship with Christ. This includes dating and close friendships.

A Christian's association with unbelievers should be only for social existence, economic existence, or to show unbelievers the way of salvation.

Many believers in today's society feel that they have a right to do whatever they want to with their own bodies. Although we may think this is freedom, it is actually enslavement to our own desires. It is fear that causes us to walk in disobedience. The fear is based on the fact that we will "miss out" on an opportunity, or that it "may not happen" again. Why is it such a fear to face the fact of losing a friendship if you don't commit sins of the flesh? This loss may be the best thing that ever happened. The friend of your dreams should be on the same page as you. This may not be the right, or best, friend for you after all.

After we become Christians, the Holy Spirit fills us and lives in us. We no longer own our bodies. "We are bought with a price," (1 Corinthians 7:23). We become Christ's slaves, which means we gain our freedom because sin no longer controls us. Being enslaved to God makes you totally free. Being enslaved to the devil (sin) puts you in bondage.

This is the very reason why we need to renew our minds to the mind of Christ, after we are born again. So that we will no longer be conformed to the patterns of this world, but we will be transformed by the renewing of our minds. Then we will be able to test and approve God's will, His good, pleasing, and perfect will for our lives (Romans 12:2).

Make the decision to renew your mind. Also, pray for strength to defeat the temptation the next time you are confronted with it. Christs' death freed us from sin, and it obligated us to His service. Because our bodies belong to God, we must not violate His standards for living.

Sexual intimacy is reserved for marriage. It is approved and blessed by God in that state. Through marriage, the husband and wife become one flesh according to God's will. The physical and emotional pleasures resulting from a faithful marriage relationship are ordained by God and held in honor by Him.

Fornication is a sin in the sight of God, and a transgression of His law. It is a snare of the enemy, and enticement to lure you into destruction. One fornicates because of the lust of the flesh. It is for self-gratification, which is the act of pleasing or satisfying oneself, especially the gratification of one's impulses, needs, or desires.

We transgress because we try to satisfy our own desires and do not consider God. We cannot leave God's Word out of the equation.

God's knowledge is critical. We lack the knowledge to understand the impact of the truth of God's Word. "For the Word is living and active, sharper than any double-edged sword. It penetrates even to dividing soul and spirit, joints and marrow; it judges the thoughts and attitudes of the heart," (Hebrews 4:12).

The Word of God is living, life-changing, and dynamic as it works in us. God's Word reveals who we are and what we are not. It goes to the core of our moral and spiritual life. It discerns what is in us, both good and evil. The demands of God's Word require decisions. We cannot just listen to the Word. We must let it shape our lives.

Some Consequences of Fornication by Brian C. Thomas:

(1) Unwanted pregnancy is a result of sex before marriage. Most young ladies are not prepared for pregnancy outside of marriage. If people would save sex until marriage, there would not be the need for a movement to legalize abortion, which is sin. Abortion came as a result of man trying to cover up sin.

(2) Statistics show that in the U.S. over 65 million people have a viral STD, with nearly 19 million new cases yearly.

(3) Fornication is one of the reasons why 50% of marriages end in divorce. Many people go into marriage with wounded emotions, spirits, and diseased bodies.

(4) When you fornicate, you sin against your own body and against a possible future spouse.

(5) If you are a woman, you may desire to have kids someday. However, 100-150,000 women each year become infertile, as a result of STDs.

If you do not become infertile, some of the STDs can cause your child to be born with defects, such as blindness. Your child should not have to suffer because of your disobedience to God.

(6) When you fornicate you defile God's Holy temple as we saw earlier in 1 Corinthians 6:19. This is the same as breaking into God's church and vandalizing the sanctuary. You would not think of doing that, would you?

If you should fall into temptation, do not be condemned. Once you know the truth, let it transform you. If you should fall, know God will be there to pick you up!! Amen

Chapter 2: Description Of The Works Of The Flesh
FORNICATION REVIEW

1. What is fornication?

____

____

____

2. God cannot be separated from His _________________________.

3. The body is not for fornication, but for the_________________.

4. When you commit fornication you sin against your own

____

5. As a Christian, your body is the personal dwelling place of the

____.

6. Just as children imitate their parents, we should imitate

____.

7. Sexual desires and activities must be placed under

____.

8. God created sex for _______________________________________, and ____ as an expression of love between

____and____.

9. Even though Christians may indulge in activities like idolatry, adultery, male prostitution, drunkenness, etc. their lives can be changed by _________________

____

10. _________________________is always striving to gain control of us.

11. We cannot always prevent temptation, but there is a way of
____ (1 Corinthians 10:13).

12. After we become Christians the ____
____ lives inside of us.

13. Being enslaved to God make you ____,
but being enslaved to the devil puts you into ____.

14. After we are born again, we need to ____
our mind with the Word of God.

15. After marriage the husband and wife become_________________________ flesh.

16. Fornication is a ____ in the sight of God.

17. Fornication is for _________________________-_________________________
which is the act of pleasing or satisfying oneself.

18. Name at least 3 consequences of fornication:

____

____

____

____

19. If we should fall into temptation, we will be condemned.
(Circle the answer) True or False

IDOLATRY

The Merriam Webster Dictionary defines idolatry as the worship of a physical object as a God. Immoderate attachment or devotion to something.

In the Old Testament, idolatry was attractive to the Israelites. The Israelites were surrounded by heathen nations who believed that the worship of several gods was superior to the worship of a single God. In other words, more was better. God's people were influenced by these nations, and constantly imitated them instead of obeying God's command to keep themselves holy and separate from them.

The gods of the other nations did not require the kind of obedience that the Lord God of Israel demanded. For instance, many of the pagan religions included sexual immorality with temple prostitutes as part of their religious rituals. This appealed to many within Israel. God, on the other hand, required His people to obey His high moral standards as defined in His Law to maintain a saving relationship with Him. They had to resist the tendency toward immorality, and other sinful practices condoned or blessed by the pagan religions.

Because of the demonic character of idols, idolatry sometimes produced genuine and demonstrable results for those who worshipped idols. The demonic powers behind the idols were able, though on a limited basis, to impart temporary material and physical benefits. Fertility gods promised the birth of children, weather gods (sun, moon, rain, etc) promised the appropriate conditions for abundant crops, while warrior gods promised protection from enemies and victory in battle. Such benefits were attractive to the Israelites, and for this reason they were willing to serve these idols.

The New Testaments call covetousness a form of idolatry (Colossians 3:5). People who are not satisfied with what they have, but are greedy for more, will not hesitate to give their allegiance to the principles and desires of those who can get them what they want. Even though such people may not worship gods made out of wood and stone, they do worship the demons that stand behind greed and covetousness. Thus, they are Idolaters.

Scripture condemns idolatry because it distorts the truth and leads people away from God. God will not tolerate any form of idolatry. He frequently warned against it in the Old Testament. The New Testament also warns against idolatry. It manifests itself in many forms today. It appears in the false world religions, as well as in sorcery, Satanism, and other forms of the occult. It is found where men and women give themselves over to greed and materialism, rather than trusting in God alone.

This occurs within the church when people believe that they can serve God, and experience His salvation and blessings, while at the same time participate in the immoral and wicked practices of the world. The New Testament admonishes us not to be greedy, covetous, or immoral.

We should keep our lives free from the love of money and be content with what we have, because God has said, "Never will I leave you; never will I forsake you." So, we say with confidence, "The Lord is my helper, I will not be afraid. What can man do to me?" (Hebrews 13:5-6). "Flee from all forms of idolatry," (1 Corinthians 10:14).

In today's society, we allow many things to become gods to us. Money, fame, work, objects, or pleasure can become gods to us when we concentrate too much on them for personal identity, meaning and security.

The cares and worries of this life, and the deceitfulness of wealth choke out the Word of God, making it unfruitful (Matthew 13:22). We become so consumed with what we have, and what we don't, that we blot out the Word of God and it becomes of non-effect, producing no fruit of righteousness.

"For the love of money is a root of all kinds of evil," (1 Timothy 6:10). Some people, eager for money, have wandered from the faith and pierced themselves with many griefs. Greed leads to all kinds of evil; marriage problems, robbery, blowups in partnerships, separation from God, or an inability to see God. To master greed, you must control it at the root. Get rid of the desire to be rich. Do not make an idol out of money or things. Desire to seek God and let Him give you the desires of your heart.

Of course, no one sets out with the intention of worshipping these things, but it happens. By the amount of time we devote to these things, they grow into gods that control our thoughts and our energies. Allow God to hold the central place in our lives, which will keep these things from turning into idol gods.

Do not be deceptive by saying you love God. You trust Him, yet you make no attempts to study His Word, listen to His teachings, pray or fellowship with other believers. Do not profess your allegiance to God and His Word, while at the same time giving equal or greater allegiance to persons, institutions, traditions, or authorities on earth. Do not allow people or things to become the focus of your values, desires, and dependence. Doing this will eventually displace your reliance on and faith in God Himself.

Whomever, or whatever, you give all your time and energy to, that is the person or thing that you are worshipping. Are you spending time with God by studying His Word? "Do your best to present yourself to God as one approved, a workman who does not need to be ashamed and who correctly handles the word of Truth" (2 Timothy 2:15). We should build our lives on His Word and build His Word into our lives, because it alone tells us how to live for and serve Him. Studying God's Word is vital. Otherwise, we will be lulled into neglecting God and our true purpose for living.

Throughout the process of maturing, you will encounter many trials and tests. They come to grow you spiritually. The Word of God says, "Count it all joy when you face trials of many kinds, because the trying of your faith develops perseverance, stability," (James 1:2). As you face trials, do not focus on the trials, focus on God knowing that the trial will pass. Trust God with all your heart and lean not to your own understanding. Acknowledge Him in all your ways and He will direct your path (Proverbs 3:5-6).

CONSEQUENCES OF IDOLATRY BY 2CHERISH2COMMEND:

(1) Idolatry arouses God's displeasure. Idolatry is the most heinous injury and affront to the true God. It is transferring his worship and honor to a rival.

(2) Idolatry brings physical ruin, brokenness, pain, suffering, death, and judgment.

(3) We are made in God's image, and when we idolize someone or something else it reduces God in our lives. He should have first place in our lives. He made us for His purpose and pleasure.

We can do nothing on our own. We need God to fight our battles. We can do all things through Him because He strengthens us (Philippians 4:13). Turn your hardships into times of spiritual growth and maturity. Jesus came and died for us that we would have life, and have it more abundantly (John 10:10). God is the only way, truth, and the Life (John 14:6). Eternal life is Christ's life in us.

IDOLATRY REVIEW

1. **What is idolatry?**

   ____

   ____

   ____

2. **The demonic powers behind the idols in the Old Testament were able to impart temporary** ___________________________________ **and** _____________________ **benefits.**

3. **These benefits were attractive to the Israelites and for this reason they were willing to serve** _____________________________________**.**

4. **The New Testament calls** _________________________ **a form of Idolatry, (Colossians 3:5).**

5. **Why does scripture condemn Idolatry?**

   ____

   ____

   ____

6. **"**___________________________________ **from all forms of Idolatry," (1 Corinthians 10:14).**

7. **What are three things in today's society that we allow to become gods to us:**

   ____

   ____

8. "For the _______________________________ of money is the root of all Evil," (1 Timothy 6:10).

9. Allow _______________________________ to hold the central place in your life, which will keep things from turning into idol gods.

10. We should build our lives on God's _______________________________and build His Word into our lives.

11. Trials and tests come to grow us up_______________________________.

12. "My brethren, count it all joy when you fall into divers temptations; knowing this, that the trying of your _______________________________ worketh patience," (James 1:2-3).

13. Name two consequences of Idolatry:

____

____

14. Jesus came and died for us, so we would have life and have it more __________ ____, (John 10:10).

HATRED

The Merriam Webster Dictionary defines hatred as intense hostility and aversion usually deriving from fear, anger, or sense of injury. Extreme dislike or disgust.

In our culture, hatred is primarily perceived as an emotion. However, in scripture, the emphasis is often on volition (a choice or decision made by the will). One who hates decisively rejects something or someone.

God's hatred is distinctive from human hatred. It is always directed against evil and God's hatred is not an overpowering emotion, but is always balanced by His love, compassion, mercy, holiness, and other attributes.

Scripture affirms that God hates evildoers (Psalm 5:6), pagan worship (Deuteronomy 12:31), practices like lying and perjury (Proverbs 6:16-19), and injustice (Micah 3). This means that God detests and rejects each of these things. Thus, the godly person will hate what God hates (Psalm 139:21), and will love what God loves.

When human hatred is addressed in scripture, it is portrayed as a destructive emotion to be avoided. Hatred as active animosity flows from man's sinful nature (Galatians 5:20), and it is associated with violence (Proverbs 29:10). Jesus explains that the divine law against murder is a condemnation of hate-filled anger, for anger motivates violence and revenge (Matthew 5:21, 22).

For instance, Haman in the book of Esther, is a prime example of human hatred. Haman was Prime Minister of Persia under King Xerxes. He was a very arrogant leader. He measured his self-worth by the power or influence he thought he had over others. He respected King Xerxes as his superior, but he could not accept anyone else as an equal.

Haman's pride was wounded when Mordecai, a minor government official, refused to kneel to him as he passed. Because of this, Haman became consumed with hatred for Mordecai.

He was already filled with racial hatred for the Jewish people, because of the longstanding hatred between the Jews and Haman's ancestors, the Amalekites. Mordecai was dedicated to God and refused to give homage to any human person. This challenged Haman's self-centered religion. Haman considered the Jews as a threat to his power, and he wanted to kill the entire race.

Through a series of events involving Queen Esther and Mordecai, Haman's plot to kill the Jews was thwarted. He suffered the fate that was intended for Mordecai and his people. Haman was hanged on the gallows that he had built for the Jews. He risked everything for an evil purpose and lost. Evil (hatred) does not pay. This is one of the lessons to be taught concerning this evil sin. The very punishment that is intended for another person may happen to you if you operate out of an evil heart. Hatred will be punished.

Haman's pride stimulated anger and hatred toward those who would not flatter him. It distorted his perspective that he was willing to kill an entire race of people because of one person's slight. The evil plans of the enemy will backfire. He will eventually shoot himself in the foot. When Haman acted on his anger, he set in motion a series of events that destroyed himself, not Mordecai. A thirst for power and prestige is self-destructive.

As Christ followers, we are called to love one another, not to hate. We are to "love our enemies, bless them that curse us, do good to them that hate us and pray for those who despitefully use us and persecute us," (Matthew 6:44). Vengeance belongs to God, who alone can punish justly (Hebrews 10:30). By rejecting hatred in favor of love, we (believers) will "not be overcome by evil, but we will overcome evil with good," (Romans 12:17-21).

Hatred plays a major role in our society today. One nation hates the other nation, father hates his son, a son hates his father, a daughter hates her mother, one race hates another race; this should not be. This is sin. People are not aware of the impact this evil sin has on their lives. The consequences just do not add up to the devastation that the sin of hatred can cause.

We hate one another and don't even know why, or we hate each other because we think someone has done something to us that they didn't even do. We must get a hold of ourselves and renew our minds to the things of God before it is too late. The hatred you feel for someone may have stemmed from an emotion, but it is a serious heart condition.

"Christ loved the church and gave Himself up for her to make her holy, cleansing her by the washing with water through the word, and to present her to Himself as a radiant church, without stain or wrinkle or any other blemish, but holy and blameless," (Ephesians 5:25-27). We are His Church. Christ's death sanctified and cleansed us from the old ways of sin and set us apart for His sacred service.

We hurt ourselves when we hate. Often, the person we hate does not even know that he/she is being hated. The person who hates becomes depressed or even comes to the point of hurting themselves, because they are so hurt. Don't let this sin enslave you to the point of destroying yourself, because this is what it was designed to do. "The thief cometh, not but to steal, kill and destroy; Jesus came that you would have life more abundantly," (John 10:10). He cannot destroy you, but he will lead you to destruction, if you listen to him. Hatred is a sin, let it go. Free yourself from this attack of the enemy and go forward. Choose life.

THE CONSEQUENCES OF HATRED BY EVERYDAY HEALTH

Everydayhealth.com

1. Hate is a strong emotion. This mental venom can pollute your spirit, poison your soul, and seep into all the relationships that surround you. It can be damaging and mind-consuming.

2. Hate can be explosive (outward) when turned towards others, and this can be dangerous and ugly. It can motivate violent crime and destructive behavior. Hatred can also be implosion (inward) towards self. Both of these will eat you up inside. The more you feed it, the stronger it becomes. It will cause you to hurt yourself or someone else.

Diffuse your hatred by:

- Stopping to take a deep breath when you feel anger. Let it out very slowly and repeat this process for four or five repetitions.

- Consciously challenging your irrational hateful thoughts

- Replacing those hateful, irrational thoughts with calmer rational thoughts.

- Limiting your contact with a person who hateful feelings are directed towards.

- Employing a "distraction strategy" to refocus your mind—watch a movie, go for a walk, read a book, exercise.

HATRED REVIEW

1. **What is hatred, according to The Merriam Webster Dictionary?**

____

____

____

2. **In our culture hatred is perceived as an_______________________________________.**

3. **A person who hates decisively _______________________________________
    something or someone.**

4. **God's hatred is not an overpowering emotion but is balanced by His
    _______________________________, _______________________________________,
    mercy, _______________________________________, and other attributes.**

5. **Scripture affirms that God hates _______________________________________,
    pagan worship, practices like lying and perjury, and**

____

6. **When human hatred is addressed in scripture, it is portrayed as a destructive
    emotion to be avoided.**

    (Circle the correct answer) True or False

7. **Anger motivates _______________________________________ and revenge.**

8. **In the book of Esther, who is a prime example of Hatred?**

____

9. **As Christ followers, we should** ____
   one another and not hate.

10. **Hatred is a serious** _____________________________________**condition.**

11. **Name one consequence of hatred?**

____

____

12. **Name at least one way to diffuse hatred:**

____

____

***Hatred stirs up conflict, but love covers all wrongs, (Proverbs 10:12).**

***Whoever conceals hatred with lying lips and spreads slander is a fool, (Proverbs 10:18).**

ADULTERY

According to The Merriam Webster Dictionary, adultery is voluntary sexual intercourse between a married person and someone other than that person's current spouse or partner.

The Bible teaches the following concerning adultery: It is a transgression of God's moral law. Transgress means to violate or sin. In the Old Testament adultery was punished by death.

Adultery can bring permanent and serious consequences. "But whoso committeth adultery with a woman lacketh understanding: he that doeth it destroyeth his own soul. A wound and dishonor shall he get; and his reproach shall not be wiped away," (Proverbs 6:32-33).

"At the window of my house I looked out through the lattice. I saw among the simple, I noticed among the young men, a youth who lacked judgment. He was going down the street near her corner, walking along in the direction of her house at twilight, as the day was fading, as the dark of night set in.

Then out came a woman to meet him dressed like a prostitute and with crafty intent. (She is loud and defiant, her feet never stay at home; now in the street, now in the squares, at every corner she lurks). She took hold of him and kissed him and with a brazen face she said:

I have fellowship offerings at home; today I fulfilled my vows. So I came out to meet you; I looked for you and have found you! I have covered my bed with colored linens from Egypt. I have perfumed my bed with myrrh, aloes and cinnamon.

Come, let's drink deep of love till morning; let's enjoy ourselves with love! My husband is not at home; he has gone on a long journey. He took his purse filled with money and will not be home till full moon.

With persuasive words she led him astray. She seduced him with her smooth talk. All at once he followed her like an ox going to the slaughter, like a deer stepping into a noose till an arrow pierces his liver, like a bird darting into a snare, little knowing it will cost him his life," (Proverbs 7:6-23).

Even though this young man does not know where he is going, the adulteress knows where she wants him. These are the strategies the adversary uses to trap you. Notice she was dressed in a way to allure men. She is very bold. She invited him over to her place. She persuaded him with smooth talk. She cunningly answered his every objection. She traps him leading to his death literally or figuratively.

To resist temptation, make sure your life is filled with the Word and the Wisdom of God. Recognize the snares and enticements of the enemy and run swiftly away from them. Guard your mind by not reading pornographic books, looking at seductive pictures, or encourage fantasies that stimulate the wrong desires. Stay away from those people (so called friends) that tempt you to sin.

Do not focus on the present moment but focus on the future. "Today's thrill can lead to tomorrow's ruin." Do not allow sexual sin to lead to sorrow, regret, or death.

Adultery is a grave and detestable sin against God and against the innocent partner who has been defrauded. The shame and disgrace of that sin remains with the guilty party for life. Though the guilt of adultery may be forgiven, its reproach will remain. Its scars and wounds will take a period of time to heal.

Adultery is a sin of such magnitude and consequence that it gives the innocent person the right to end the marriage by divorce. Although divorce is a tragedy, marital unfaithfulness is such a cruel sin against one's mate that Christ states that the innocent party has a proper right to end the marriage. He or she is free to marry another believer (1 Corinthians 7:27-28).

The seriousness of adultery is rooted in the biblical view of marriage as a covenant between two people, who reflect the relationship of God with His people. Within the covenant relationship, each party owes the other complete and exclusive faithfulness. Only by remaining faithful to the covenant relationship can both partners be blessed.

CONSEQUENCES OF ADULTERY BY LESLI WHITE (1-4)

1. Guilt and shame—These two are big components of adultery, for the one who cheats and the wounded spouse. It is embarrassing to both parties, and they will usually try to hide the fact from others. This is true for the cheating spouse and for the innocent person. He or she may feel tainted or may feel like, "There must be something wrong with me." Life becomes constricted.

2. **Loss of Trust and Intimacy–An entangled affair is always a result of an intimacy deficient marital relationship. The freedom to be oneself, to be accepted and appreciated, is important to identify what was missing in the marital relationship, and repair the loss.**

3. **Divorce–Cheating may not always end in divorce, but it can have a devastating impact. It is probably the most damaging thing that can happen in a marriage. Such negative emotions can be hard to put behind you, and many feel that there is no way to rebuild trust in the marriage. Negative emotions will fade with time and life will become normal again, but most people deal with infidelity in the marriage by divorce.**

4. **Illness–Sexually transmitted diseases. When a partner cheats, illness can occur. Being cheated on is already a miserable experience, but contracting a disease and bringing it back home to the innocent person can be devastating.**

5. **Pregnancy–When you cheat on your spouse, pregnancy can occur. An unwanted child can be produced.**

6. **If the woman/man is married, her spouse might attempt to bring harm.**

ADULTERY REVIEW

1. **The Merriam Webster Dictionary says that "Adultery is ________________ ________________________ sexual relations of a ________________________ ________________ person with someone other than his or her lawful spouse."**

2. **____ means to violate or sin.**

3. **Stay away from people or friends who tempt you to**

   ____

4. **Adultery is a sin of such magnitude and consequence that it gives the innocent person the right to end the marriage in**

   ____

5. **Marriage is a covenant between two people:**

   Circle the answer: True or False

6. **Guard your mind by reading pornographic books, looking at seductive pictures, etc.**

   True or False

7. **Name two consequences of Adultery:**

   ____

   ____

"For the lips of the adulterous woman drip honey, and her speech is smoother than oil; but in the end she is bitter as gall, sharp as a double-edged sword. Her feet go down to death; her steps lead straight to the grave. She gives no thought to the way of life; her paths wander

aimlessly, but she does not know it. Now then, my sons, listen to me; do not turn aside from what I say. Keep to a path far from her, do not go near the door of her house, lest you lose your honor to others and your dignity to one who is cruel, lest strangers feast on your wealth and your toil enrich the house of another. At the end of your life you will groan, when your flesh and body are spent. You will say, 'How I hated discipline! How my heart spurned corrections! I would not obey my teachers or turn my ear to my instructors. And I was soon in serious trouble in the assembly of God's people.' Drink water from your own cistern, running water from your own well. Should your springs overflow in the streets, your streams of water in the public squares. Let them be yours alone, never to be shared with strangers. May your fountain be blessed, and may you rejoice in the wife of your youth. A loving doe, a graceful deer—may her breasts satisfy you always, may you ever be intoxicated with her love. Why, my son, be intoxicated with another man's wife? Why embrace the bosom of a wayward woman? For your ways are in full view of the Lord, and He examines all your paths. The evil deeds of the wicked ensnare them; the cords of their sins hold them fast" (Proverbs 5:3-22).

STRIFE

According to The Random House Dictionary, strife is vigorous or bitter conflict, discord, or antagonism; A quarrel, struggle, or clash; Competition or rivalry.

> "But if you harbor bitter envy and selfish ambition in your hearts, do not boast about it or deny the truth. Such 'wisdom' does not come down from heaven but is earthly, unspiritual, of the devil. For where you have envy and selfish ambition, there you find disorder and every evil practice," (James 3:14-16).

Bitter, envy, and selfish ambition are inspired by the devil. With the many pressures in society today, we can easily be drawn into wrong desires. Sometimes even well meaning Christians can lead us in the wrong direction, by advice like, "Assert yourself. Go for it. Set high goals." Although we should assert ourselves and set high goals, we should not allow this desire to draw us into greed and destructive competitiveness. When we seek the wisdom of God, this will deliver us from the need of comparing ourselves to others and coveting their possessions.

Strife is related to envy and refers to the vice of selfish ambition, which prompts us to promote our own interests. Selfish ambition in the Church is "earthly." It defiles that which is holy and of the spirit (sensual) or unspiritual, without the Holy Spirit; and devilish. It is inspired by demons, which are "evil spirits."

Strife among believers will always cause conflicts and disputes, which are always harmful. These quarrels result from evil desires battling within us. We want more possessions, more money, higher status, or more recognition. When we want these things badly enough, we fight to get them.

The cure for evil desires is humility. Pride makes us self-centered and leads us to conclude that we deserve all we can see, touch, or imagine. It creates greedy appetites for far more selfish desires than we need. We need to release ourselves from our self-centered desires by humbling ourselves before God, and realizing that all we really need is His approval. When the Holy Spirit fills us, we see that this world's seductive attractions are only cheap substitutes for what God has to offer.

Paul talks about strife and disputes in the church in (1 Corinthians 6:1-6). Paul explained how to handle open immorality in the congregation between believers. Society has set up a legal system where disagreements can be resolved in court. Paul declares that disagreeing Christians should resolve their differences among each other and not in the secular court system. Paul says, "As Christians, we have the Holy Spirit and the mind of Christ, so why should we turn to those who lack God's wisdom?" We should be able to handle disputes among ourselves because of the authority God gave to us as believers.

The reason Paul disagreed with taking our disputes to the secular court system were:

(1) If the judge and jury are not Christians, they are not likely to be sensitive to Christian values.

(2) The basis for going to court is often revenge, which should never be a Christian's motive.

(3) Lawsuits make the church look bad, causing unbelievers to focus on its problems rather than on its purpose.

However, Paul does indicate that the church must judge its members according to God's Word and standards when serious sin, wrongdoing, immorality, or persistent ungodly conduct is the issue. Such wicked actions demand judging and discipline for the sake of the person involved, the purity of the church, and the witness of Christ in the world.

In an instant, where a so-called "brother" has divorced or deserted his family and refused to support his wife and children with alimony, a mother with the right motives and concern for her children may take recourse in the courts. Paul is not advocating that those who break the law be allowed to defraud or threaten the life or well-being of another. He is speaking of minor disputes where the wrong could be accepted and tolerated.

Conflicts and disputes among families and friends can also be very harmful.

First, at a family gathering an argument breaks out and for years afterward, several of the family members refuse to communicate with one another.

Second, a family member becomes so angry because of a misunderstanding or miscommunication that he/she leaves home and never returns.

Should we go on continuing in strife so that grace may increase? By no means! We have died to sin-how can we live in it any longer? It doesn't matter what the conflict or dispute was about, who was right or who was wrong. We must expose the enemy, forgive, and move on. God has called us to love one another and walk in total freedom.

"For if you forgive men when they sin against us, our heavenly Father will also forgive us. But if we do not forgive men of their sins, our Father will not forgive our sins," (Matthew 6:14-15). We must forgive if our desire is to grow or move on. Those who are unwilling to forgive have not become one with Christ, who was willing to forgive even those who crucified Him.

Are you walking in strife toward a family member, friend, or anyone else? If so, lose yourself of this stronghold, and allow God to take control over the territory that the devil once possessed. "The thief came to steal, kill and destroy but Jesus came that we might have life, and that we might have it more abundantly, (John 10:10)."

CONSEQUENCES OF STRIFE BY CREFLO DOLLAR:

1. This evil spirit aims to destroy from within. It will sneak in unnoticed and cause arguments, contention, and resentment. This evil spirit can turn something healthy, thriving, and productive into something dysfunctional.

2. When things are going well, the enemy will try to cause trouble by bringing conflict into the situation.

3. Strife is one of Satan's favorite weapons, which he uses to spread anger and confusion. We are vulnerable to it when our spirits don't line up with God's Spirit.

The way to combat strife is by deliberately walking in unity and love. This includes forgiving others for hurtful things they may say or do, refusing to hold grudges, and putting others first. Self-centeredness is a root of strife, but staying out of the center and keeping God there instead changes our entire focus.

STRIFE REVIEW

1. **Define Strife:**

   ____

   ____

   ____

   ____

2. **Strife does not come from Heaven but it is earthly and comes from the**

   ____

3. **Strife is related to**

   ____

4. **Strife is inspired by** _________________________________ **which are evil spirits.**

5. **The cure for evil desires is**

   ____

6. _________________________________ **makes us self-centered and leads us to conclude that we deserve all we can see, touch, or imagine.**

7. **Paul believed that we should be able to handle disputes among ourselves (rather than taking them to the secular court system) because of the authority ________ _________________________________ give to us as believers.**

8. **God has called us to _________________________________ one another and walk in _________________________________.**

9. Memorize John 10:10:

____

____

____

____

10. Name one consequence of Strife:

____

____

11. Name one way to combat strife?

____

____

LASCIVIOUSNESS

The Random House Dictionary defines lasciviousness as inclined to lustfulness; inciting sexual desire; expressing lust or lewdness. Arousing or inciting sexual desire.

Paul describes its nature as, "Having lost all sensitivity, they have given themselves over to sensuality, so as to indulge in every kind of impurity, with a continual lust for more" (Ephesians 4:19). Some examples are men who lie with men, women who lie with women, men who lie with animals, or having sexual relationships with close family members.

This mindset can be summed up as futile, meaning emptiness, purposelessness. Your understanding has been darkened. You have been alienated from God. You are ignorant of God's way. Your heart has been hardened and an unfeeling state has taken place. The Greek word means "to have ceased to care."

As Christians, our conduct is the most effective sermon that we will ever preach. We have to reject and avoid living like the world. God has given us instructions through His Word on how we are to conduct ourselves. Thinking as the world thinks and acting as the world acts will, no doubt, lead to sensuality and impurity.

Homosexuality was widespread in Paul's day. Many pagan preachers encouraged it. Although these practices were common in pagan religions and cultures, God dealt harshly with those who began to follow them. Such practices lead to disease, deformity, and death. They disrupt family life and society and show a low regard for the value of oneself and of others. These things are taken very lightly in society today, some even trying to make them acceptable. But they are still sins in God's eyes. If you consider them acceptable, then you are not judging by God's standards.

God is willing to receive anyone who comes to Him in faith, and Christians should love and accept others regardless of their background or past. It is not a question of whether God loves you, or not. God loves you regardless of the sin you commit. The question is whether you love God enough to give up the sin. In the Kingdom of God, we must die to the flesh or die to our own sensual desire and follow God. When we follow God, it is not about us and what we want to do, but it is about God and His purpose for our life. He is the Captain of the ship, and we are just passengers.

Society does not set the standard for God's law. Many homosexuals believe that their desires are normal, and they have a right to express them. But God neither obligates nor encourages us to fulfill all our desires (even normal ones). Those desires that violate His Laws must be controlled.

One may say, "I was born this way," or "Why does God allow me to be this way?" Well, after the fall of Adam and Eve, we are born in sin. This is why we have to be "born again." Once we are born again, we have to renew our minds to the things of God. "Do not conform any longer to the pattern of this world, but be transformed by the renewing of your mind. Then you will be able to test and approve what God's will is-His good, pleasing, and perfect will," (Romans 12:2).

Renewing our mind will give us insight and truth concerning this homosexual tendency. You will not be able to conquer this sin, or any other sin, if you do not renew your mind.

In our society today we have become so lax, or loose, so that anything goes. Even confessing Christians are indulging in the sins of this new generation. Mind over matter has plunged some of us into this, "I do as I please," era of deceit. When we should be teaching others, we are still immature ourselves, thus falling prey to the enemy's attack. Instead of us renewing our mind with the Word of God , we allow the enemy to deceive us into pleasing our own selfish desires, therefore rejecting the will of God.

God actually allows us to reject Him. Romans 1:24-32 talks about people who chose to reject God. God does not usually stop us from making choices that are against His will. He lets us declare our supposed independence from Him, even though He knows that in time we will become slaves to our own rebellious choices. By doing this we will lose our freedom not to sin. Does life without God look like freedom to you? There is no worse slavery than slavery to sin.

People tend to believe lies that reinforce their own selfish personal beliefs. Today, more than ever, we need to be careful about the input we allow to form our beliefs. There is television, music, movies, and the rest of the media often presenting "sinful life-styles" and unwholesome values. We find ourselves bombarded by attitudes and beliefs that are totally opposed to God's Word. Be careful what you allow to form your opinions. The Bible is the only standard of Truth.

Don't be fooled. God's plan for natural sexual relationships is His ideal for His creation. Unfortunately, sin distorts the natural use of God's gifts. Sin often means not only denying God, but also denying the way He made us. When people say that any sex act is acceptable, as long as nobody gets hurt, they are fooling themselves. In the long-run, sin hurts people–families, individuals, and whole societies.

We have a tendency, as people of God, to worship the things God made instead of worshipping Him (The Creator).

Of course, The Devil wants us to believe that we don't need to change, or that it is impossible to change the way we feel. Just think, even though it is hard for us to do, it is just a feeling. Feelings can change but principles stay the same. Obedience is better than sacrifice. This is where your freedom is, because sin is bondage.

Ask yourself this question, "What does the Word say about the way I feel?" Study the Word of God and let Him renew your mind.

CONSEQUENCES OF LASCIVIOUSNESS

1. You could be imprisoned for indecent exposure or child molestation-depending on the crime you commit.

2. You could contract a disease.

3. You could be harmed if you molest someone's child or a close family member.

LASCIVIOUSNESS REVIEW

1. **Define Lasciviousness:**

____

____

____

____

____

2. **Paul describes Lasciviousness as having lost all sensitivity, and have given one-self over to** _____________________________.

3. **Give two examples of lasciviousness:**

____

____

____

____

____

4. **The Greek meaning of the word (lasciviousness).**

____

____

____

5. **As Christians, the most effective sermon that we will ever preach is**

____

6. **We must live like the world: True or False (Circle)**

7. **If we sin God does not love us: True or False (Circle)**

8. **Once we are born again, we need to _________________________________ our minds to the things of God.**

9. **God allows us to reject Him: True or False (Circle)**

10. **The _______________________________ is the only standard of truth.**

11. **Sin is ____.**

12. **Name one consequence of lasciviousness:**

____

____

WRATH (ANGER)

According to the Scott Foresman Advanced Dictionary, anger is the feeling of strong displeasure turned against anyone or anything that has hurt or wronged us or others.

> **"Understand (this), my beloved brethren. Let every man be quick to hear (be a listener), slow to speak, slow to take offense, and to get angry. For man's anger does not promote the righteousness of God (that standard of behavior which He requires from us).**
> **So get rid of all uncleanness and the rampant outgrowth of wickedness, and in a humble (gentle, modest) spirit receive and welcome the Word, which implanted and rooted (in your hearts), contains the power to save your souls" (James 1:19-21 Amplified).**

Here James is saying to be just as ready to listen, as you are to speak. Don't be so quick to speak or to get angry. Oftentimes, we talk so much that we neglect to hear what others are saying. This communicates to others that we think our ideas are so much more important than theirs.

In these verses, James is talking about anger that erupts after our egos are bruised, "I am hurt. My opinions are not being heard." Anger is very dangerous in a person's life, which is often covered by deceit. Someone may have done you an injustice, or someone may have hurt you, and you have a right to be angry. But we should not become angry when we are offended, neglected, or when we fail to win an argument. This is called selfish anger, and it does not help anyone.

> **"In your anger do not sin. Do not let the sun go down while you are still angry, and do not give the devil a foothold," (Ephesians 4:26-27).**

The Bible doesn't tell us that we shouldn't feel angry, but it points out that we should handle our anger properly. If it is vented thoughtlessly, we can hurt others and destroy relationships. If we bottle it up inside, we can become bitter and destroy ourselves from within. To nurse our anger will give Satan an opportunity to divide us.

Oftentimes we do not even recognize that we are walking in a spirit of anger, because it is deception. We may try to hide or ignore our anger, but it comes back to haunt us. When it comes back, we try to rationalize or explain it away, but we know that it is still there.

If we just listen to ourselves as we speak, our words will reveal hidden anger stored up in us. When we store up anger, it will grow and grow until it develops into a ferocious beast. Anger can turn into rage. Rage is out of control anger. This anger can cause many physical ailments such as headaches, hypertension, depression, ulcers, colitis, and many others.

Deaths and a large percentage of incarcerations today can be attributed to the "Spirit of anger." People become emotional, and they act before they think. Things get out of hand. It does not matter whether the actions are justified or not. Moral action, not emotion, is scripture's primary concern.

Simeon and Levi, two furious brothers, tricked and wiped out the population of a town when Shechem (the son of Hamor the Hivite) prince of the country, raped their sister (Genesis 34). Their anger was justified, but their actions were sinful (Genesis 49:5-7).

The problem with human anger is that it can have an effect on moral choices. "A hot-tempered man commits many sins," (Proverbs 29:22). Anger "only leads to evil," (Psalm 37:8). A person whose actions are motivated by anger is more likely to choose an ungodly path (James 1:19-20).

Jesus identified anger as a root of murder (Matthew 5:21,22). Killing is a terrible sin, but anger is a great sin because it also violates God's command to love. Anger here refers to a seething, brooding, bitterness against someone. It is a dangerous emotion that always threatens to leap out of control, leading to violence, emotional hurt, increased mental stress, and spiritual damage. Anger keeps us from developing a spirit pleasing to God.

"Get rid of all bitterness, rage and anger, brawling and slander, along with every form of malice," (Ephesians 4:31). Paul warns us against unwholesome language, bitterness, improper use of anger, brawling, slander, and bad attitudes toward others. Instead of displaying these bad attitudes, we should be forgiving, just as God has forgiven us. We should walk in love towards our brothers and sisters in Christ, just as God showed His love by sending His Son to die for our sins.

We need to accept personal responsibility for the way we respond to situations, rather than supposing that someone or something "made" us angry. The cure for anger is forgiveness. Forgiveness is not for the other person. It is to bring freedom to you. You have to forgive, and according to Jesus, love even your enemies (Matthew 5:43-48).

We may feel angry, but we can and must stop short of sinful acts. The New Testament teaches that even when we are truly injured by another person, we are to leave vengeance in the hands of God and to concentrate on doing good (Romans 12:19-21). The proper response is prayer, not revenge. Instead of striking back when someone hurts you, ask God to take your case, bring justice, and restore your reputation. If we practice these Biblical principles, we can master anger.

CONSEQUENCES OF WRATH:

1. Wrath causes suffering, from all types of health problems, and social problems.

2. Uncontrolled anger can result in loss of employment.

3. Loss of family

4. Incarceration

WRATH: (ANGER REVIEW)

1. **Define Anger:**

____

____

____

____

____

2. **Does a man's anger promote the righteousness of God?**

Yes or No

3. **The** _______________________________________ **has the power to save your souls.**

4. _______________________________________ **is very dangerous in a person's life, which is often covered by deceit.**

5. **In your anger do not** ____.

6. **To nurse anger gives Satan an opportunity to** ___________________________ **us.**

7. **When we store up anger, it will grow and develop into a** ___________________ ____ **beast.**

8. _______________________________________ **is out of control anger.**

9. **Name two physical ailments anger can cause:**

____

____

____

____

____

10. Anger violates God's command to ___________________________.

11. The cure for anger is ___________________________.

12. Forgiveness brings freedom to the other person:

True or False

13. Name two consequences of anger:

____

____

____

**"Do not be quickly provoked in your spirit, for anger resides in the lap
of fools," (Ecclesiastes 7:9).**

VARIANCE

The Random House Dictionary defines Variance as the state, quality, or fact of being variable, divergent, different or deviate; disagreement, dispute; quarrel; Conflict, argument, contention.

"But I urge you, brethren, by the name of our Lord Jesus Christ, that all of you be in perfect harmony, and full agreement, in what you say, and that there be no dissensions or factions or divisions among you, but that you be perfectly united in your common understanding and in your opinions and judgments. For it has been made clear to me, my brethren, by those of Choe's household that there are contentions and wrangling and factions among you," (1 Corinthians 1:10-11).

This Corinthian Church was large and diverse, and the believers favored different preachers. Because at this time, there was no New Testament, the believers depended heavily on preaching and teaching for spiritual insight into the meaning of the Old Testament. Some followed Paul, who founded their church. Some who had heard Peter (Cephas) in Jerusalem followed him. While others only listened to Apollos, an eloquent and popular preacher who had a dynamic ministry in Corinth (Acts 18:24; 19:1). Although all three preachers were united in their message, their personalities attracted different people.

At this time, the church was in danger of dividing. By mentioning Jesus Christ ten times in the first ten verses, Paul makes it clear who it is all preachers should emphasize. God's message is much more important than any human messenger.

Paul wondered whether the quarrels had "divided" Christ. This is a picture of what happens when the church (Body of Christ) is divided. With the many churches and styles of worship available today, we could get caught up in the same game of, "My preacher is better than yours." To do so would divide Christ again. But Christ is not divided, and His true followers should not allow anything or anybody to divide them. Don't let your appreciation for any teacher, preacher, or author lead you into intellectual pride. We must always be careful to center our love and loyalty on God and His Word, not on any minister or person. Our allegiance must be to Christ and to the unity He desires.

Children of God can have different viewpoints without being divisive. To agree with one another, allow for no divisions, and be perfectly united in mind and thought. A group may not totally agree on every issue, but they can still work together in harmony if they only agree on what really matters. "Jesus Christ is Lord of us all." If we can come into agreement with this, we should be able to work through the things that are of lesser importance. We should behave and speak in a manner that will bring harmony and reduce arguments. Petty differences should not divide Christians.

Be willing to work together in harmony, not only in the church, but also in our place of employment, our group fellowships, and our family relationships. Don't be so eager to be different that you bring division. Be tender-hearted and humble minded, with love and peace in the forefront of every situation you encounter. Be a person that people enjoy being around, and do not bring discord to what could be a time of enjoyment.

CONSEQUENCES OF VARIANCE:

1. **Marital Stress**

2. **Divorce**

3. **Family separations**

4. **Stress disorders in a person's life**

5. **Variance can cause a hostile work environment**

VARIANCE REVIEW

1. Variance is a state of being:

____

____

____

2. In the Corinthian Church Paul, Peter, and Apollos were united in their messages, but their _________________________________ attracted different people.

3. Paul made it clear that the preachers should emphasize __________________ ______________________________________ in their messages.

4. Christ was divided?   True or False

5. We should center our love and loyalty on _________________ and His Word.

6. Jesus Christ is Lord of us _______________________________________.

7. Petty differences should not divide Christians:

True or False

8. Name three consequences of being divisive or being different:

____

____

____

____

____

EMULATIONS

The Random House Dictionary defines emulation as an effort or desire to equal or excel others; Jealous rivalry; Competition.

> "Now Israel loved Joseph more than all his children, because he was the son of his old age: and he made him a coat of many colors.
> And when his brethren saw that their father loved him more than all his brethren, they hated him and could not speak peaceably unto him.
> And Joseph dreamed a dream, and he told it to his brethren: and they hated him yet the more.
> And he said unto them, Hear, I pray you, this dream which I have dreamed:
> For behold we were binding sheaves in the field, and lo, my sheaf arose, and also stood upright; and behold, your sheaves stood round about, and made obeisance to my sheaf.
> And his brethren said to him, 'Shalt thou indeed reign over us? Or shalt thou indeed have dominion over us?' And they hated him yet the more for his dreams, and for his words," (Genesis 37:3-8).

In Josephs' day everyone had a robe or cloak. Robes were used to warm oneself, to bundle up belongings for a trip, to wrap babies, to sit on, and even to serve as security for a loan. Most robes were knee length, short sleeved, and plain. In contrast, Joseph's robe was probably the kind worn by royalty; long sleeved, ankle length, and colorful. The robe became a symbol of Jacob's favoritism toward Joseph, ahead of his brothers.

Joseph's brothers were already angry over the possibility of being ruled by their youngest brother. Joseph put fuel on the fire by having an immature, boastful attitude. No one enjoys a braggart. Joseph learned this the hard way. His angry brothers sold him into slavery to get rid of him. They sold him to the first camel caravan that passed by.

Sometimes in families there are favorites, but the divisive effects should be minimized. In a family one child may be favored over another, because he/she does not cause as much drama as the other child. Even though you may not be able to change your feelings toward the favored child, you can change your actions toward the other child.

This passage of scripture also expresses a symptom of the spirit of jealousy. In this day of fierce competition, in the business world and in the sports arena, this spirit is largely overlooked. Yes, we should be goal oriented and we should strive to do our best job in whatever we do. However, do not let your drive to be the best "drive" you in unnatural ways. This is what happened with Joseph and his ten older brothers. This spirit of competition got out of hand.

Today in the sports arena, namely football, basketball, and tennis, this spirit is obvious. You have players who try to injure opposing players in the name of "trying to win" the game. They are so concerned about winning the game, they lose sight of good sportsmanship. They have this saying that states, "Winning is not important, it is everything." Some players cannot accept the thought of losing. They must realize that somebody has to lose, and somebody has to win. They feel that if they are playing, they are playing to win. This spirit is an overachiever's spirit, and it can get more competitive than we realize.

This competitive spirit can be transferred to other areas of our lives which can result in consequences that are tragic. Imagine being married to a person with this spirit. Imagine being in a relationship, or just a friendship, with someone who has this spirit. They have an attitude of never wanting to lose at anything, neither a game nor an argument, etc. This is unnatural, and would become a miserable relationship.

When we notice such symptoms working in our life, it is important to take action against them before they gain total control of us.

The love of God is the only deterrent against this competitive spirit. "And live a life of love, just as Christ loved us, and gave Himself for us as a fragrant offering and sacrifice to God," (Ephesians 5:2).

If this become a problem, ask God for forgiveness for allowing this attitude or competitive spirit to control you. Bind it in the name of Jesus and lose the love of Christ in its place. Then live in resistance to its attempt to return. Stand firm on the resistance, because the spirit will try to return. You have to prove that you have rejected that particular lifestyle.

CONSEQUENCES OF EMULATIONS:

1. Being jealous when someone else achieves something you feel like you should have achieved will lead to an angry spirit, and cause all kinds of evil.

2. An overachiever's spirit can lead you into a snare and cause you to harm another or do something that may cause you to be harmed.

3. You will never grow past your insecurities if you always compete with someone else (in trying to take what they are doing and do it better yourself). Use the gift God has given you.

EMULATIONS REVIEW

1. **Define Emulations:**

____

____

____

2. **Should you favor one child over the other?**

> **Yes   No (circle)**

3. **What is the only deterrent against a jealous, competitive spirit?**

____

4. **Give two consequences of a competitive, jealous spirit:**

____

____

____

____

____

Bonus: Give an example of a competitive or jealous spirit that you have experienced in your life: (20 lines)

____

____

____

____

DRUNKENNESS

According to The Merriam Webster Dictionary drunkenness is, the habitual or excessive drinking of intoxicants. The condition of being drunk.

Dependence on alcohol where there is always a strong need or craving to drink is known as alcoholism. When the craving for alcohol is indulged, it leads to loss of control where the person lacks the ability to limit their drinking. They become physically dependent, and if they don't consume alcohol they goes into withdrawals. There are symptoms like sweating, shaking, nausea, and even anxiety. A person addicted to alcohol will build a tolerance for the substance, wherein they need to drink greater amounts in order to get drunk.

Due to the effect it has on our minds, bodies, and emotions alcohol is considered a drug. One fact about alcoholism is that more people die from alcohol addiction compared to those who are addicted to other drugs. Alcohol is usually used by young people so that they can cope better with the pressures, like peer pressure, and mental and physical pressures they are undergoing.

When intoxicated, alcoholics are less likely to focus or pay attention. Teen alcohol use kills 4,700 people each year. They die mostly from car crashes or other violent deaths. That's more than all illegal drugs combined. Drunk driving costs the United States more than $199 billion every year.

While alcohol and caffeine are the two most widely used substances in the world, alcohol affects an individual in the sense that it relaxes and lowers the inhibitions of a person. Generally, females who are intoxicated are more likely to engage in sex with a stranger. If the people who drink, are addicted, or dependent on alcohol, have mental disorders (like anxiety and depression) it's even harder to get a diagnosis, because alcoholism masks these emotional problems.

Stats on Alcoholism also state that people who are intoxicated are more likely to attempt suicide. Once an adolescent is addicted to alcohol, it's highly possible that a taste for drugs and other addictions will occur too. Some of the facts about alcohol addiction can be found at: Alcohol Facts and Statistics: (www.niaaa.nih.gov), National Institute on Alcohol Abuse and Alcoholism-National Institutes of Health.

ALCOHOL USE IN THE UNITED STATES:

Prevalence of Drinking: According to the 2015 National Survey on Drug Use and Health (NSDUH), 86.4 percent of people ages 18 or older reported that they drank alcohol at some point in their lifetime. 70.1 percent reported that they drank in the past year. 56.0 percent reported that they drank in the past month.

Prevalence of Binge Drinking and Heavy Alcohol Use: In 2015, 26.9 percent of people ages 18 or older reported that they engaged in binge drinking in the past month. 7.0 percent reported that they engaged in heavy alcohol use in the past month.

ALCOHOL USE DISORDER (AUD) IN THE UNITED STATES:

Adults (ages 18+): According to the 2015 NSDUH, 15.1 million adults ages 18 and older (6.2 percent of this age group) had AUD (Alcohol Use Disorder). This includes 9.8 million men (8.4 percent of men in this age group) and 5.3 million women (4.2 percent of women in this age group).

About 6.7 percent of adults who had AUD in the past year received treatment. This includes 7.4 percent of males and 5.4 percent of females with AUD in this age group.

Youth (ages 12-17): According to the 2015 NSDUH, an estimated 623,000 adolescents ages 12-17 (2.5 percent of this age group) had AUD in the past year received treatment. This includes 5.1 percent of males and 5.3 percent of females with AUD in this age group.

ALCOHOL-RELATED DEATHS:

An estimated 88,000 people (approximately 62,000 men and 26,000 women) die from alcohol-related causes annually, making alcohol the third leading preventable cause of death in the United States. The first is tobacco. The second is poor diet and physical inactivity.

In 2014, alcohol-impaired driving fatalities accounted for 9,967 deaths (31 percent of overall driving fatalities). An alcoholic's life-span is shortened by 10-12 years.

An unlimited number of statistics on alcoholism are available because of the great number of alcohol-related health problems, fatalities, and injuries that are experienced by or caused by those who are alcohol dependent.

Neither the Old nor New Testaments forbid the use of intoxicants, but each book makes it clear we are not to drink to excess. Christians are to surrender control of their lives to God's Spirit (Ephesians 5:18), not to alcohol. In every situation, choices exist. No person is forced to choose against his or her will, and we must assume responsibility for our choices.

> "They promise them freedom, while they themselves are slaves of depravity; for a man is a slave to whatever has mastered him," (2 Peter 2:19)."

Peter is talking about false prophets and teachers who promised the people freedom, while they were corrupt themselves. Freedom to them meant doing anything they wanted to do. No one is ever completely free in that sense. If we refuse to follow God, we will follow our own sinful desires and become enslaved to what our bodies want. If we submit our lives to Christ, He will free us from slavery to sin. Christ frees us to serve Him, a freedom that results in our ultimate good.

CONSEQUENCES OF BEING AN ALCOHOLIC:

1. Drinking alcohol excessively will cause you to have a shorter attention span.

2. Lack of fine motor coordination

3. Impaired judgment

4. Loss of memory and lack of comprehension

5. Delayed motor reactions

6. Balance problems and ataxia (affects the nervous system)

7. Blurred vision and sensation impairment

8. In and out of consciousness or complete unconsciousness

9. Amnesia during the events while intoxicated

10. Staggering gait

11. Vomiting with aspiration

12. Respiratory depression

13. Incontinence of urine

14. Slowed heart rate

15. Comatose

16. Severe decrease in heart rate

17. Lack of pupillary response to light

18. Life-threatening respiratory depression

19. Higher self-confidence

20. Death

21. Incarceration

22. Cirrhosis of the liver and many other health problems

DRUNKENNESS REVIEW

1. **What is Drunkenness?**

____

____

____

____

____

____

2. **Alcoholism is a dependence on** ___________________________

____

3. **When a person becomes physically dependent on alcohol, and he cannot obtain it for some reason, what happens?**

____

____

____

____

4. **Because of the effect of alcohol on our mind, body, and emotions it is considered a** _______________________________.

5. **Name a reason why young people use alcohol?**

____

____

____

____

---

6. Alcoholics are likely to be more attentive when they drink.

True or False

7. After an adolescent is addicted to alcohol they are more likely to try other drugs.

True or False

8. According to www.niaaa.nih.gov., how many people die from Alcohol annually?________________________________

9. According to this study an alcoholics' life-span is shortened by about 10 years.

True or False

10. Name five consequences of being an alcoholic:

____

____

____

____

____

____

____

____

____

ENVYINGS (JEALOUSY)

According to The Random House Dictionary, envy is a sense of discontent or jealousy with regard to another's advantages, success, possessions, etc. Desire for an advantage possessed by another.

"And Abel brought of the first-born of his flock of the fat portions. And the Lord had respect and regard for Abel and his offering. But for Cain and his offering He had no respect or regard. So Cain was exceedingly angry and indignant, and he looked sad and depressed. And the Lord said to Cain, why are you angry? And why do you look sad and dejected? If you do well, will you not be accepted? And if you do not do well, sin crouches at your door. It's desire is for you, and you must master it. And Cain said to his brother, 'Let us go out to the field.' And when they were in the field Cain rose up against Abel, his brother, and killed him," (Genesis 4:4-8).

The Lord accepted the offering of Abel because he came before God in true faith and dedication to righteousness (Hebrews 11:4). He offered a blood sacrifice and he had the right attitude. Cain's offering was rejected because he lacked a sincerely obedient faith, and because his deeds were evil. God takes pleasure in our offerings and thanksgivings only when we are striving to live a righteous life according to His will (Deuteronomy 6:5).

The sin in this case was envy. "Bitter envy and selfish ambition," which are inspired by the devil. Cain was envious of his brother in this passage because God was pleased with Abel's offering and not his. We must master the sin of envy because "sin" is crouching at the door, and it desires to possess you. For Cain to master the sin lurking at the entrance to his desires, he would have to give up his jealous anger, so that sin would not find a foothold in his life.

When we walk in the sin of envy, we are thinking only of our own selfish desires. Not once do we consider the other person, but we are only thinking of ourselves. We envy another because we feel as if we will miss out on something, or that we will never be able to do what we see someone else doing. You do not have to envy or desire what someone else has or what someone else is doing, because God will fulfill every desire you have if you just seek Him.

"Do not fret because of evil men or be envious of those who do wrong; for like the grass they will soon wither, like green plants they will soon die away," (Psalm 37:1-2). We should never envy evil people, even though some may be extremely popular or excessively rich. No matter how much they have, it will fade and vanish like grass that withers and dies. Those who follow God live differently from the wicked, and they will have far greater treasures in heaven. What the unbeliever gets may last a lifetime if he is lucky. What we possess from following God will last forever.

If the achiever is a believer, we should not envy them, but thank God for their success. If we can appreciate what God is doing through the lives of our brothers and sisters in Christ, then He can also do a mighty work in our lives.

Because of our fallen nature, we have a tendency toward the sin of envy. This evil desire we cannot ignore, but we have to deal with it decisively. We have to nail this sinful nature to the cross. This does not mean that we will never see traces of this evil desire again. As Christians, we still have the capacity to be tempted with this sin, or any other sin, but we have been set free from the power of sin over us and no longer have to give in to it. Everyday we must commit our sinful tendencies to God's control, crucify them daily, and moment by moment draw on the Spirit's power to overcome them.

Humble yourself before God. "God resists the proud but gives grace to the humble," (James 4:6). Pride makes us self-centered and leads us to conclude that we deserve all that we can see, touch, or imagine. It creates greedy appetites which far exceeds what we need. We can be released from our self-centered desires by humbling ourselves before God.

As we draw closer and closer to God, we will desire what He desires. Our evil desires will diminish. We will love righteousness, and we will hate evil, just like our Father.

God pictures sin as a tempting force or power which, like a wild beast or demon, is ready to attack and to devour. Yet God also ascribes to human beings the capacity to overcome and to resist sin by submitting to His Word, with the assistance of His Grace. The Holy Spirit will help us master the sin of envy. Seeking God's wisdom delivers us from the need to compare ourselves to others and to want what they have. It is our choice whether we will yield to sin, or whether we will conquer it (Romans 6). This will be a lifelong battle that will not end until we are face-to-face with Christ.

CONSEQUENCES OF BEING ENVIOUS (JEALOUSY) BY HTTP://WWW.NCREALITIES. WORDPRESS.COM

1. Jealousy will bring hopelessness and depression (You may feel hopeless and depressed because other unsaved people seem to have greater achievements than you). Your dreams and visions may be delayed, but not cut off. Don't give up. You will not be disappointed.

2. Jealousy will make you cruel. Jealousy will add hardness to your life. With jealousy in your life, you are in the worst possible situation you can be in.

3. Jealousy causes you to have limited power. You will always be comparing yourself with someone else. When you compare, you belittle what God has done. Jealousy projects the image of selfishness. Be happy when others get blessed.

4. Jealousy brings bitterness. This will result in stress, cancer, and premature death. Bitterness is a slow suicide.

5. Jealousy brings confusion. All sorts of evil and bad practices come from jealousy. It's the root of murder, confusion, disorder, and uncertainty. It is the foundation of every evil thing.

ENVYINGS (JEALOUSY) REVIEW

Define Envy (Jealousy)?

1. ____

   ____

   ____

   ____

2. **"Bitter envy and selfish ambition" are inspired by the**

   ____

3. **Sin is crouching at our door and its desire is to** _____________

   ____

4. **When we walk in jealousy we are thinking about others.**

   True or False

5. **What we possess from following God will last** ________________.

6. **James 4:6 states, "God resists the proud but gives Grace to the humble."**

   True or False

7. **Pride makes us self-centered. True or False**

8. **Sin is a life-long battle, but it will end before we see Christ.**

   True or False

9. Name two consequences of being Jealous:

____

____

____

____

____

____

HERESIES

The Random House Dictionary defines heresies as, religious opinion or doctrine at variance with the orthodox or accepted doctrine. The willful and persistent rejection of any article of faith by a baptized member of the church. Any belief or theory that is strongly at variance with established beliefs, mores, etc.

"For false Christs and false prophets shall rise, and shall show signs and wonders, to seduce, if it were possible, even the elect," (Mark 13:22). Believers today must be aware that within the churches there may be preachers, ministers, and pastors of God's Word who are of the same spirit and life as the corrupt teachers of God's law in Jesus' day, (Matthew 24:11,24). Jesus warns us that not everyone who professes Christ is a true believer, neither are all Christian writers, missionaries, pastors, evangelists, teachers, deacons, and workers are who they claim they are.

These Ministers, etc. will "outwardly appear righteous unto men," (Matthew 23:28). They come in "sheep's clothing," (Matthew 7:15). They may base their message on God's Word, proclaiming high righteous standards. They may appear sincerely concerned for God's Work and Kingdom, showing great interest in the salvation of the lost, professing love for all people. They may appear to be great ministers of God, commendable spiritual leaders, anointed by His Holy Spirit. They may perform great miracles and have great success, with multitudes following them.

Nevertheless, these people find their spiritual ancestors in the false prophets of the Old Testament [Jeremiah 14:14 (Hosea 4:15)], and in the Pharisees of the New Testament. Away from the crowds and in their private lives, the Pharisees were given over to "extortion and excess" (Matthew 23:25), "full of dead men's bones, and of all uncleanness," (Matthew 23:27) and, "full of hypocrisy and iniquity," (Matthew 23:28). Their lives behind closed doors involved such things as lust, immorality, adultery, greed, and self-centered indulgence.

These imposters attain a place of influence in the church in two ways. Some false teachers/preachers begin their ministry in sincerity, truth, purity, and genuine faith in Christ. Then, because of their pride and immoral desires, their personal commitment and love for Christ gradually die.

Consequently, they are severed from the Kingdom of God and became instruments of Satan while disguising themselves as Ministers of righteousness (2 Corinthians 11:15).

Other false teachers/preachers are never genuine believers in Christ. Satan has planted them within the church from the very beginning of their ministry (Matthew 13:24-28, 36-43), using their ability and charisma, aiding in their success. His strategy is to place them in influential positions, so that they can undermine the genuine work of Christ. If they are discovered or exposed, Satan knows that great damage will come to the gospel and that the name of Christ will be put to open shame.

> "But there were also false prophets among the people, even as there will be false teachers among you, who will secretly bring in destructive heresies, even denying the Lord who bought them, and bring on themselves swift destruction" (2 Peter 2:1).

Jesus told the disciples that false teachers would come (Matthew 24:11). Peter had heard these words, and at this time, he saw them come true. Just as false prophets had contradicted the true prophets in the Old Testament times (Jeremiah 23:16-40), telling people only what they wanted to hear, false teachers were twisting Christ's teachings and the words of His Apostles. These teachers were belittling the significance of Jesus' life, death, and resurrection. Some claimed that Jesus couldn't be God. Others claimed that He couldn't have been a real man. These teachers allowed, and even encouraged all kinds of wrong and immoral acts, especially sexual sin.

We must be careful to avoid false teachers today. Any book, tape series, or TV message must be evaluated according to God's Word. Beware of special meanings or interpretations that belittle Christ and His work.

Peter warns of immoral and greedy false teachers, who will use people as a means of reaching their own selfish goals. These false teachers are more interested in making money than in teaching truth. Peter and Paul both condemned greedy, lying, teachers (1 Timothy 6:5). Before you send money to any cause, evaluate it carefully. Is the teacher or preacher clearly serving God or promoting his/her own interests? Will the money be used to promote valid ministry, or will it merely finance further promotions?

The New Testament indicates that deceptive teachers will characterize the church age, and that their activities will increase "in latter times," (Matthew 24:11). The "latter times" began with Christ's resurrection and will continue until His return, when He will set up His Kingdom and judge all humanity.

False teachers always were and still are a threat to the church. Jesus and the apostles warned against them. The danger Timothy faced in Ephesus seemed to have come from certain people in the church, who were following some Greek Philosophers. They taught the body was evil and that only the soul mattered. The false teachers refused to believe that the God of creation was good, because His very contact with the physical world would have soiled Him. These Greek influenced church members honored Jesus, but they could not believe He was truly human. Paul knew that if their teachings were left unchecked, they would greatly distort Christian truth.

It is not enough that a teacher appears knowledgeable, is disciplined and moral, or even says he/she is speaking for God. If his words contradict the Bible, his teaching is false. We have to guard against any teaching that causes believers to dilute or reject any aspect of their faith.

Satan deceives people by offering a clever imitation of the real thing. The false teachers gave stringent rules (such as forbidding people to marry or to eat certain foods). This made them appear to be self-disciplined and righteous. Their strict discipline for the body, however, could not remove sin. We must not be so impressed by a teacher's style or credentials that we fail to look at his teaching about Jesus Christ. His conclusions about Christ show the source of his message.

The believer's protection against such deception involves utter loyalty to God and His inspired Word, and the knowledge that men of great charisma and anointing can be deceived, and then deceive others with their mixture of truth and error. This awareness must be accompanied by a true desire within the believer's heart to do the will of God and to walk in righteousness and the fear of God.

Discern people by their character. Do they have a sincere and pure devotion to God? Do they manifest the fruit of the Spirit (Galatians 5:22-23), love sinners (John 3:16), hate evil and love righteousness (Hebrews 1:9), and cry out against sin (Matthew 23:1-12)? Discern the person's motives. True Christian leaders will seek to honor Christ (Philippians 1:20), lead the church into sanctification (Acts 26:18), save the lost (1 Corinthians 9:19-22), and proclaim and defend the Gospel of Christ and the Apostles (Philippians 1:17).

Examine the person's reliance on scripture. This is a key issue. Does he believe and teach that the original writings of both the Old and New Testaments are fully inspired by God, and that we are to submit to all their teachings (2 John 9-11). If not, we can be assured that the teacher and his message are not of God.

Check the person's integrity with respect to the Lord's money. Does he handle all finances with integrity, and responsibility, seeking to promote the work of God in ways consistent with the New Testament standards for leaders (1Timothy 3:3; 6:9-10).

We must understand that in spite of all that a faithful believer can do in evaluating a person's life and message, there will still be false teachers within the churches who, with the help of Satan, remain undetected until God decides to expose those persons for what they are.

God has promised that during the "last days" He will save all who call upon His name, and separate themselves from this perverse generation (Acts 2:16-21). He will pour forth His Spirit on them.

CONSEQUENCES OF HERESY:
FROM–AGAINST HERESIES T-HERESIES.BLOGSPOT.COM

What are the Effects of Heresy?

1. Heresy brings confusion for unbelievers, since they hear several different and contradictory voices all claiming to be telling them the authentic good news.

2. Heresy brings trouble for the Church. Unless false teachers are silenced, as Paul tells Titus that they should be, they will ruin households and upset the faith of some (Titus 1:11). Genuine believers can be unsettled by the teaching of these men (2 Tim. 2:18). In addition to this damage, false teachers also drain the time, energy, and resources of churches when they are not dealt with. Drawn out conflicts with false teachers can divert and distract gospel churches from evangelism and the planting and nurturing of new congregations.

3. Heresy places those who embrace it, and refuse to be corrected, in danger of eternal condemnation. At the very least the salvation of those who are deceived by gospel denying error cannot be affirmed. There is hope that God may grant such people repentance. But the apostles did not shrink back from spelling out the danger of turning to a "different gospel." Paul makes it clear that whether the "false brother," an angel from heaven, or even the apostles themselves preach another gospel than the one that Paul had preached, then they should be accursed (Gal. 1:6-9).

Harold Brown summed up the consequences of truth and error by saying, "Just as there are doctrines that are true, and that can bring salvation, there are those that are false, so false that they can spell eternal damnation for those who have the misfortune to be entrapped by them."

HERESY REVIEW

1. **Define Heresy?**

____

____

____

____

____

____

____

____

2. **Everyone who professes Christ is a true believer.**

True or False

3. **Some false teachers/preachers are never genuine believers in Christ.**

True or False

4. **Some false teachers/preachers begin their Ministry in sincerity, truth, purity, and genuine faith in Christ.**

True or False

5. **Satan's strategy for planting false prophets in influential positions is so they can undermine the genuine work of**

____

6. **If they are discovered or exposed, Satan knows this will cause great damage to the** ____
and that the name of Christ will be put to shame.

7. **Did Jesus tell the disciples that false teachers would come?**

Yes or No

8. **Are there still false prophets today?**

Yes or No

9. **Name two effects or consequences of Heresy:**

____

____

____

____

____

____

____

____

REVELING OR REVELRY

The Random House Dictionary defines reveling as, to make merry; indulge in boisterous festivities; Boisterous merrymaking or festivity. To take great pleasure or delight.

The biblical word reveling refers to rowdy, disorderly parties that go late into the night and consist of drinking, feasting, and other bad behavior. Reveling requires alcohol or drugs to fuel its passions. It arises from a human nature of being out of control.

> "The night is nearly over; the day is almost here, so let us put aside the deeds of darkness, and put on the armor of light. Let us behave decently, as in the daytime, not in orgies and drunkenness, not in sexual immorality and debauchery, not in dissension and jealousy. Rather, clothe yourselves with the Lord Jesus Christ and do not think about how to gratify the desires of the sinful nature" (Romans 13:12-14).

The night refers to the present evil time. The day refers to the time of Christ's return. Some people are surprised that Paul lists dissension and jealousy with the gross and obvious sins of orgies, drunkenness, and sexual immorality. Like Jesus in His Sermon on the Mount (Matthew Chapters 5-7), Paul considers attitudes as important as actions. Just as hatred leads to murder, so jealousy leads to strife and lust to adultery. When Christ returns, He wants to find His people clean on the inside, as well as on the outside.

Clothe ourselves with the Lord Jesus Christ by first being baptized (Galatians 3:27). This shows our solidarity with other Christians and with the death, burial, and resurrection of Jesus Christ. Let us exemplify the qualities Jesus showed while He was here on earth (love, humility, truth, service). In a sense, we role play what Jesus would do in our situation (Colossians 3:10-17). We must not give our desires any opportunity to lead us to sin. Avoid situations that could open the door to gratifying our sinful desires.

Sodom and Gomorrah were major targets for self-deception. They gave themselves over to the enemy, showing no signs of resistance (Genesis 19). Sodom and Gomorrah were two of five "cities of the plain," a fertile area in Abraham's time, which lay at the southern end of the Dead Sea.

Abraham's nephew, Lot, allured by the wealth of the area, chose to settle in Sodom when he separated from his uncle. Lot failed to consider the moral corruption of the population, illustrated by the attempted homosexual rape by the men of Sodom of angelic messengers sent to Lot (Genesis 19:1-5). Because of their wickedness (Genesis 18:22), the cities were destroyed in a firestorm of divine judgment, probably through the agency of an earthquake and ignition of deposits of highly flammable bitumen found in the area.

Sodom and Gomorrah are synonymous in scripture with vice and depravity. The prophets speak the name of these cities as a curse when describing a morally corrupt generation of Israelites (Isaiah 1:10; Jeremiah 23:14). Sodom also serves as an example of God's commitment to judge sin (Amos 4:11; Matthew 10:15; Jude 7). The fall of Sodom and Gomorrah, along with the flood, epitomize the biblical conviction that God is holy and surely will punish those who persist in wickedness.

Satan will use anything necessary to trap us in his web of deceit. He will use the difficult times that we go through as weaknesses against us. We sometimes turn to unhealthy relationships, substance abuse, wild parties, pornography, cheating, gossiping, lying, or anything that will take our mind off our problems. The dangerous thing here is the fact that alcohol and drugs can be life altering substances. Once you begin to indulge in these activities, it may take 20-30 years to walk away from them. The consequences that come with the longevity of the use of these substances, can be detrimental.

One can be lured into doing things he/she may not have done if the mind was "sober." Bad decisions are made, and people's minds are clouded. When one's mind becomes altered with substance or drug abuse, secrets are revealed that otherwise would have been kept confidential. The body's organs can be destroyed as a result of long-term drug or substance abuse.

The most dangerous thing with indulging in substance and drug abuse is that the person may forsake his/her relationship with the living God. Perhaps you were saved and delivered previously, but end up falling back into temptation once again. Now there is a great possibility that you may find yourself arrested, jobless, or even incarcerated. Can you imagine what this could do to one's faith walk?

Give careful consideration before indulging into any recreation that has the ability to alter a person's behavior in such a way that causes him or her to lose control. A few moments of pleasure is not worth a lifetime of pain.

We must rid ourselves of the evil practices of immorality. Commit ourselves to the teachings of Christ. Get rid of the "old life" and put on the "new life," which is in Christ Jesus and guided by the Holy Spirit.

What does it mean to "put on the new self?" Our conduct should match our faith. If you are a Christian, act like one. To be a Christian means more than just making good resolutions and having good intentions. It means taking the right actions. This is a straight-forward step that is as simple as putting on your clothes.

We, as Christians, are all in a continuing education program. The more we know about Christ and His work, the more we are being changed to be like Him. This process is lifelong, therefore, we must keep learning and obeying Godly principles. There is no justification for drifting along, but there is an incentive in finding the rich treasures of growing in Him. It takes practice, ongoing review, patience, and concentration to keep in line with His will.

Think before you act. Turn to God, and renew your mind in the things of God. If you are saved, you have been washed clean by Jesus' blood. He died and shed His blood so we could live.

CONSEQUENCES OF REVELING:

1. Many mistakes with lifelong consequences are made during seasons of reveling. For example, overindulgence in alcohol or drugs could lead to incarceration, or in some cases, death.

2. During the times of reveling, one could engage in illegal activities that lead to the murder of another person.

3. One could contract a disease or terminal illness during these wild parties that involve a lifetime of pain and regret.

REVELING REVIEW

1. **What does the word Reveling entail?**

____

____

____

____

____

____

2. **We must not give our desires an opportunity to lead us into**

____

____

3. **We should indulge in situations that open the door to gratifying our sensual desires.**

True or False

4. **Why were the cities of Sodom and Gomorrah destroyed?**

____

____.

5. **_______________________________________ will use anything to trap us in his web of deceit.**

6. **Name two things that we may do when we go through difficult times:**

____

____

____

____

____

7. **The body organs can be _______________________**
    as a result of long-term drug or substance abuse.

8. **What does it mean to "put on the new self?"**

____

____

____

____

____

9. **Name one consequence of Reveling:**

____

____

____

____

____

____

____

SEDITIONS

The Random House Dictionary defines Seditions as an incitement of public disorder or rebellion against government; An action in speech or writing promoting such disorder or rebellion; Rebellious disorder.

> "Now I beseech you brethren, mark them which cause divisions and offences contrary to the doctrine which ye have learned; and avoid them" (Romans 16:17).

Paul gives a strong warning to the church in Rome to be alert to all those who do damage to the church by corrupting and distorting the "doctrine" (teaching) of Paul and the other apostles. They were to "Mark" the proponents of false doctrine and "avoid them" and their ministry. Those marked may have been antinomians (against the law), who taught that because salvation is by grace. Saving faith does not necessarily include obedience to Christ Jesus (Ephesians 4:14). They believed that a person could live in sin and reject God's moral law, yet possess eternal salvation.

These false teachers were eloquent orators, speaking with comforting words and flattering speeches (Jude 16), deceiving simple Christians.

After Paul sent his personal greetings to Romans and Greeks, Jews and Gentiles, men and women, prisoners and prominent citizens, he stated, "I urge you, brothers, to watch out for those who cause divisions and put obstacles in your way that are contrary to the teaching you have learned. Keep away from them. For such people are not serving our Lord Jesus Christ, but their own appetites. By smooth talk and flattery they deceive the minds of naive people. Everyone has heard about your obedience, so I am full of joy over you; but I want you to be wise about what is good, and innocent about what is evil. The God of Peace will soon crush Satan under His feet" (Romans 16:17-20).

Just as Paul warned the people in his day to keep away from people or anything that causes them to doubt the Word of God, we should also keep away from such people. When we read books or listen to sermons, we should check the content of what is written or said, and not be fooled by smooth style.

Christians who study God's Word will not be fooled, even though superficial listeners may easily be taken in (Romans 16:17-20). Some people believe everything they hear or read. Unfortunately, many ideas printed and taught are not true.

Christians should have faith, but they should not be gullible. Verify every message you hear, even if the person that brings it says it is from God. If the message is truly from God, it will be consistent with Christ's teachings.

The people in Berea opened the scriptures for themselves and searched for truths to verify or disprove the message they heard, (Acts 17:10-12). Always compare what you hear with what the Bible says. A preacher or teacher who gives God's true message will never contradict, or explain away anything that is found in God's Word.

"Warn them before God against quarreling about words; it is of no value, and only ruins those who listen. Do your best to present yourself to God as one approved, a workman who does not need to be ashamed and who correctly handles the Word of Truth. Avoid godless chatter because those who indulge in it will become more and more ungodly. Their teaching will spread like gangrene. Among them are Hymenaeus and Philetus, who have wandered away from the truth. They say that the resurrection has already taken place, and they destroy the faith of some. Nevertheless Gods' solid foundation stands firm, sealed with this inscription: The Lord knows those who are His, and, 'Everyone who confesses the name of the Lord must turn away from wickedness'" (2 Timothy 2:14-19).

Paul urged Timothy to remind the believers not to argue over unimportant details (quarreling about words), or have foolish discussions (godless chatter), because such arguments are confusing, useless, and even harmful. False teachers loved to cause strife and divisions by their meaningless quibbling over unimportant details. Paul had handed Hymenaeus over to Satan (removed him from the fellowship of the church), because his false teaching concerning the resurrection was destroying some people's faith. Paul did this so Hymenaeus would see his error and repent. The ultimate purpose of this punishment was correction.

The false teachers were denying the resurrection of the body. They believed that when a person became a Christian he or she was spiritually reborn, and that was the only resurrection there would ever be. To them resurrection was symbolic and spiritual, not physical. Paul taught that believers would be resurrected after they die, and that their bodies as well as their souls will live eternally with Christ (2 Corinthians 5:1-10; 1 Thessalonians 4:15-18). We cannot shape the doctrines of Scripture to match our opinions. If we do so, we put ourselves above God. Our beliefs should be consistent with God's Word.

To handle the word of truth correctly, we must study what the Word of God says so we can understand what it means. Do not indulge in theological quarreling, because it is ruinous and almost never helpful. Avoid being drawn into arguments or quarrels. Learn how to persuade others to believe and practice truth, but do so gently and kindly. Do not be deceived by jargon or religiosity. Look for true spiritual power and godliness in others.

Try to avoid debates and arguments over certain topics in Bible Study that have a tendency to leave everyone disgusted and upset. The Word of God should never be debated.

Separate yourselves from people who argue and debate over the Bible. Wherever you see these debates, you will find the spirit of pride. Pride is an arrogant behavior or conduct, an exaggerated idea of one's dignity or importance. The Word of God is truth and not someone's opinion of what a certain topic means. Study the Word and know God for yourself, and then you can rightfully divide it.

CONSEQUENCES OF SEDITIONS:

1. Debating or arguing about the Word of God can cause arguments and confusion.

2. Raising objections over trivial matters can cause strife and divisions.

3. Some people can easily be deceived by false teachers because they believe everything they hear.

SEDITIONS REVIEW

1. **Define Seditions:**

____

____

____

____

____

____

2. **Verify every message you hear, even if the person that brings it says it is from God.**

   True or False

3. **A preacher or teacher who gives God's true message will never contradict or explain away anything that is found in God's Word.**

   True or False

4. **Everyone who confesses the name of the Lord must turn away from**

____

5. **Our beliefs should be consistent with God's** _________________________.

6. **Theological quarreling is** _________________________________
   and almost never _________________________________.

7. **Avoid being drawn into** _________________________________
   or _________________________________.

8. Name one consequence of Seditions:

____

____

____

____

____

MURDER

The Revell Bible Dictionary defines murder as the personal, intentional killing of another human being, in contrast to accidental homicide or causing the death of another person in war or in defense of one's property.

In the King James version of the Bible, Deuteronomy states, "Thou shall not kill." The Amplified Bibles states, "You shall not murder." You may say, "I don't murder people." Good. That fulfills the letter of the law. But Jesus explained that hateful anger breaks this commandment, (Matthew 5:21-22).

Have you ever been so angry with someone who may have mistreated you, and for a moment you wished that person were dead? Have you ever fantasized that you could do someone in, or murder someone? Jesus' teaching concerning this law demonstrates that we are capable of murder in our hearts. We may be legally innocent, but we are all morally guilty of murder. We should commit ourselves to love and reconciliation, rather than anger and hatred.

Jesus teaches about anger. He states, "You have heard that it was said to the people long ago, do not murder, and anyone who murders will be subject to judgment. But I tell you that anyone who is angry with his brother will be subject to judgment," (Matthew 5:21-23).

When Jesus said, "But I tell you," he was not doing away with the law or adding his own beliefs. He was giving a fuller understanding of why God made the law in the first place. For example, Exodus 13, when Moses said, "You shall not murder," Jesus taught that we should not even become angry enough to murder because we have already committed murder in our hearts. When the Pharisees read this law, not having literally murdered anyone, they felt righteous. Yet they were angry enough with Jesus that they would soon plot His death. A death which they would not do the dirty work themselves. We often miss out on the intent of God's Word when we read his rules for living without trying to understand why He made them. Do you keep God's rules but close your eyes to His intent?

Of course, killing is a terrible sin, but anger is a great sin too. God commands us to love one another. Anger violates this commandment.

> "This is the message you heard from the beginning: We should love one another. Do not be like Cain, who belonged to the evil one and murdered his brother. And why did he murder him? Because his own

actions were evil and his brothers' were righteous. Do not be surprised if the world hates you. We know that we have passed from death to life because we love our brothers. Anyone who doesn't love remains in death. Anyone who hates his brother is a murderer, and you know that no murderer has eternal life in him," (1 John 3:11-15).

Cain killed his brother Abel when God accepted Abel's offering and not his (Genesis 4:1-16). Abel's offering showed that Cain was not giving his best to God, and Cain's jealous anger drove him to murder. People who are morally upright expose and shame those who aren't. When we live for God, the world will hate us because we make them painfully aware of their immoral way of living.

"Looking diligently lest any man fail of the grace of God; lest any root of bitterness springing up trouble you and thereby many be defiled" (Hebrews 12:15).

Like a small root that grows into a big tree, bitterness springs up in our hearts and overshadows even our deepest Christian relationships. It refers to a spirit and attitude that is characterized by intense animosity and resentment. A "bitter root" comes when we allow disappointment to grow into resentment, and when we nurse grudges over past hurts. Bitterness brings jealousy, dissension, and immorality. If we do not control this strongman, it will lead to murder.

There are far too many killings or murders in our society today. Bitterness is the root cause. Even though you may have been abused or hurt at some stage of your life, do not allow bitterness to come and set up camp in your life.

"The weapons of our warfare are not carnal, but mighty through God to the pulling down of strong holds; Casting down imaginations, and every high thing that exalteth itself against the knowledge of God, and bringing into captivity every thought to the obedience of Christ; And having in a readiness to revenge all disobedience, when your obedience is fulfilled," (2 Corinthians 10:4-6).

You do not want to commit the sin of murder in your heart, because this displeases God. It is the total opposite of God's law to love. The physical act of murder could land you in prison for a number of years, life, or even capital punishment. Practice self-control and thought control. Think before you act.

"The thief cometh not, but for to steal, and to kill, and to destroy" (John 10:10). The thief is the devil, whose main goal is to get you out of society, so he can destroy your purpose. You have a purpose for being on Earth, whether you believe this or not. If he can cause you to miss out on discovering who you really are, he has accomplished his goal.

"Vengeance is mine; I will repay, saith the Lord" (Romans 12:19). Let go, and let God bring your enemy to his knees and force him to admit his wrongdoings. God has all the facts about the person or the situation that the enemy is using to destroy you. Pray for the person who hurt you, and trust God to fight your battle.

CONSEQUENCES OF MURDER

1. A life sentence in prison or even the death penalty.

2. You can murder people with your mouth by lying about them, or just scorning their name. By doing this you could cause a person to lose his/her job. You can cause bodily harm to another person by scorning their name.

3. You can cause loss of friendship by being untruthful.

MURDER REVIEW

1. **Define murder according to the Revell Bible Dictionary:**

____

____

____

____

____

____

____

____

____

____

2. **We should commit ourselves to _______________________ and reconciliation, rather than _______________________ and hatred.**

3. **God commands us to love one another. _______________________ violates this commandment.**

4. **We know that we have passed from_______________________ to life because we love our brothers.**

5. **Anyone who hates his brother is a _______________________.**

6. **What drove Cain to murder his brother Abel?**

____

7. **When we live for God the world will love us:**

True or False

8. **Like a small root that grows into a big tree** ________________________________ **springs up in our hearts and overshadows our deepest Christian relationships.**

9. **What is one of the root causes of killings and murders in our society today?**

____

10. **John 10:10 says, "The thief cometh not but to** ________________________________ ,

____ **, and**

____

11. **Vengeance belongs to us: True or False**

12. **Pray for the people who hurt you and let** ________________________________ **fight your battles.**

13. **Name one consequence of murder:**

____

____

____

WITCHCRAFT

The Random House Dictionary defines witchcraft as, The art or practices of a witch; sorcery, magic. Magical influence. Witchery.

Sorcery is connected with the occult, which includes contact with the dead, supernatural powers, paranormal energies, or demonic forces in order to acquire power to manipulate or influence things or people.

A witch is a person who is supposed to have the ability to manipulate evil powers by magic. The "witch of Endor" in (1 Samuel 28) was a medium, who claimed she had contact with the spirit world.

Because of this, Saul had banned all mediums and spiritualists (those who consulted with the dead) from Israel. But when he could not get an answer from God himself, out of his desperation, he turned to a medium for counsel. He had removed the sin of witchcraft from the land, but not from his heart. We should be sure that when we denounce sin, we also change our heart condition. If we don't, the sin will return. Denounce means to publicly declare to be wrong or evil.

Saul was so overwhelmed at the sight of the Philistine army that he turned to the occult. As we confront difficulties and obstacles in our lives, we should turn to God and depend upon Him. Turning to anything else will lead to disaster.

God had strictly forbidden the Israelites to have anything to do with divination, sorcery, witchcraft, mediums, spiritualists, or anyone who consults with the dead (Deuteronomy 18:9-14). Sorcerers were to be put to death (Exodus 22:18). When people could not get an answer from God, they turned to pagan gods.

Saul had the "witch of Endor" call Samuel back from the dead to ask Samuel what he should do about the Philistines who were fighting against him. God sent the spirit of Samuel to appear to Saul. Mediums do not really contact the dead, but usually communicate with deceiving spirits. The medium was shocked and terrified when Samuel appeared. Samuel's appearance revealed to her that she was dealing with a power far greater than she had known before. She did not call Samuel by trickery, or the power of Satan. God brought Samuel back to give Saul a prediction regarding his fate, a message Saul already knew. This in no way justifies efforts to contact the dead or communicate with persons or spirits from the past, because God is against all such practices (Galatians 5:19-21).

God did not answer Saul's appeals because Saul had not followed His previous directions. Because of Saul's disobedience, the next day, God handed him over to the Philistines. Saul and his sons were killed. Sometimes we wonder why God has not answered our prayers. Have we fulfilled all the responsibilities that He has already given us? Don't be surprised when He doesn't give further guidance.

We also see the same thing taking place in our society today. There have been reports of certain authorities who've used the art of fortune-telling (tarot cards), when they could not locate a missing person. There are also some people in today's society who make frequent visits to the fortune teller to find out what their future holds.

Practitioners of the occult have Satan and demons as the source of their information. God does not reveal His will to them. Instead, He speaks through His own channels of the Bible, His Son Jesus Christ, and the Holy Spirit.

Religious cults can also be seen as witchcraft. There are two kinds of cults. The first being a manipulative group who controls its members completely and demands complete commitment and loyalty. The second kind of cult is one who deviates from Biblical Christianity.

Basically, what makes a religious group a cult is a denial of the essential doctrines of the Christian faith. For example, denial of the deity of Jesus Christ or the Trinity, denial of Jesus' resurrection, denial of salvation by faith, etc.

Another distinguishing factor of cults is the way they twist the Bible, and interpret it incorrectly. Many cults take verses out of context, combine passages that aren't relevant to each other, and use incorrect definitions of theological terms.

These theological teachings are presented to people slowly, and the thinking process of the person is gradually changed. As the audience hears the doctrine presented repeatedly, they gradually accept points one at a time.

Christian leadership can be led by manipulation, intimidation, and domination. The members are controlled by the spirit of fear. The leaders require absolute loyalty from their members. Members are removed from their prior lives altogether, including their jobs, families, and homes. The Word of God is slightly twisted to the point that it is very difficult to discern.

The intimidation causes you to take your eyes off God and focus on the leader. You will begin to see him as God. This strategy is used to alter your thinking. One thought is changed at a time to lunge you into the enemy's way of thinking. This will cause you to lose sight of the promises of God and be defeated.

We are told to test the spirits, to see whether they are from God.

Many false prophets have gone out into the world, (1 John 4:1-3). This is how you can recognize the Spirit of God. Every spirit that acknowledges that Jesus Christ has come in the flesh is from God, but not every spirit acknowledges Jesus is from God. This is the spirit of antichrist, which you have heard is coming and even now is already in the world.

There is an article on www.allaboutcults.org on the topic of Religious Cults. Many may ask a question or want to know, Why does it matter? Why can't we all get along? Contrary to their historical foundations of deeming Christendom to be misguided, evil, or apostate, most of the cults are now claiming to be Christians themselves. They declare the divine authority of the Bible, but they manipulate the scriptures to suit their own purposes.

Although religious cults may claim to serve Jesus Christ, and may use Christian terminology, their doctrines are dangerously different. Why is this an issue? Because these organizations don't lead to the Jesus Christ of the Bible, but to a false prophet and gospel message altogether. If these religious groups are based on bad history, bad doctrine, or bad motives, then we must respectfully expose these shortcomings. If these religious cults are presenting false teachers, then multitudes of people are being led astray.

To the believer, God is the truth and the life. A person who maintains a personal covenant relationship with God relies on Him for all things. To rely on magic, sorcery, drugs, demonic spirits, mediums, or any form of witchcraft is to abandon God. To practice witchcraft is to turn to supernatural powers, which are less than, and essentially hostile to God and His word. The Gospel of Christ challenged first-century men and women not only to turn to God, but to turn away from idols and from the world view that idolatry represents (1 Thessalonians 1:9).

On our path to purpose, we will encounter some places and circumstances that we may question ourselves. How or why did I get here? Each experience we undergo is leading us to our destiny. There may be some obstacles ahead of us that cause us to detour, or go in a roundabout way to reach our destination. We may find ourselves in a wilderness experience. In a wilderness experience, there is a lesson to be learned, but do not stay in the wilderness so long. Turn and proceed back onto the path to destiny.

Being in the wilderness too long will cause you to become stagnant (stop developing) or bitter. You must not allow the enemy to hold you captive. Because your hope is in Christ, you can let go of the past experiences. Look forward to becoming who God desires for you to become. Press toward the goal to win the prize for which God has called you in Jesus Christ (Philippians 3:14).

"Count it all joy when you persevere through the wilderness experiences because the trying of your faith will build stability and endurance" (James 1:2-3).

CONSEQUENCES OF WITCHCRAFT:

1. These are familiar spirits that are being led by Satan.

2. These spirits are deceptive and are not of God.

3. You will walk in error if you follow these spirits.

4. These spirits can be utilized by demons to draw people into a satanic web.

5. Some of the games that your children play can teach young people how to cast spells and contact spirit guides.

WITCHCRAFT REVIEW

1. Define Witchcraft:

____

____

____

____

____

____

____

____

2. A ____
is a person who is supposed to have the ability to manipulate evil powers by magic.

3. Denounce means to publicly declare something to be wrong or

____

4. As we confront difficulties and obstacles in our lives, who should we turn to?

____

5. Practitioners of the occult have ____
and ____ **as the source of their information.**

6. What channels do God speak through?

____

____

____

____

____

____

7. Religious cults can also be seen as witchcraft:

True or False

8. What makes a religious group a cult?

____

____

____

____

9. What does the intimidation spirit cause one to do?

____

____

____

10. Name two consequences of witchcraft:

____

____

____

____

____

____

____

COMMENTS ON THE WORKS OF THE FLESH

"For he who sows to his own flesh (lower nature, sensuality) will from the flesh reap decay and ruin and destruction; but he who sows to the Spirit will from the Spirit reap life eternal" (Galatians 6:8 Amplified Bible).

"For God so loved the world that He gave His one and only Son, that whoever believes in Him shall not perish but have eternal life. For God did not send his Son into the world to condemn the world but to save the world through Him. Whoever believes in Him is not condemned, but whoever does not believe stands condemned already because he has not believed in the name of God's one and only Son.

This is the verdict: Light has come into the world, but men loved darkness instead of light because their deeds were evil. Everyone who does evil hates the light and will not come into the light for fear that his deeds will be exposed. But whoever lives by the truth comes into the light, so that it may be seen plainly that what he has done has been done through God," (John 3:16-21).

Sin is the greatest enemy to the human race, destroying one's soul and life. Through the atoning death of Jesus, and the sanctifying power of the Holy Spirit, those who turn to Jesus will be made free from the guilt and slavery of sin.

Chapter 3:

RELEASING OUR FAITH

—⟡—

"In the beginning GOD created the Heavens and the Earth" (Genesis 1:1). God created the heavens and the earth as manifestations of His glory, majesty, and power. As we look at the entire created cosmos, from the immense expanse of the created universe to the beauty and order of nature, we cannot help but stand in "awe" of the majesty of the Lord God, our creator.

God created the Heavens and the Earth in order to receive back the glory and honor due Him. All of the elements of nature, trees of the forest, snow and rain, flowers and the trees, the sun and the moon, the stars rivers and streams, hills and mountains, animals and birds, etc.—shout praises to the God that made them. God desires and expects to receive our praise in a greater measure.

God created the Heavens and Earth in order to provide a place where His purpose and goals for humankind might be fulfilled. God created Adam and Eve in His image so that He could have a loving, personal relationship for all eternity.

As Children of God, we must understand that GOD is good. "Every good and perfect gift is from above, and cometh down from the Father of Lights, with whom is no variableness, neither shadow of turning" (James 1:17 Amplified Bible).

Understand that God is only capable of doing good. He can only do good. He will never change. He is the same yesterday, today, and forever (Hebrews 13:8). He will always keep His promises.

"God is a perfect God." He cannot and will not make an error. God is infallible, which means He is exempt from liability or error. He is absolutely trustworthy.

"God is Love." He does not just love us, but He is Love! "For God so loved the world that He gave His only begotten Son" (John 3:16). God gave His Son as an offering for sin on the cross. He was not forced to do this. He did it because of His great love for us. This verse reveals God's Heart and purpose. His Love is so great that it can embrace all people. He watches over and cares for His Creation.

When interpreting God's historic acts, scripture ascribes appropriate qualities or attributes to Him. According to scripture, God is Spirit. He is one, yet exists in three persons as Father, Son, and Holy Spirit. He is the Creator and Sustainer of the universe. He is loving, holy, just, and good. He is a Judge and Avenger. He is righteous, forgiving, full of mercy, full of pity. He has purposes and carries out His purposes. He is wise, immortal, eternal. He is all-powerful, a refuge, a help in time of trouble. He is a Father to those who trust Him.

God is the one who hears and answers prayer. He delivers and rescues. He is a Law-giver and Life-giver. He is our rock, our shield, our fortress, our strong tower, our glory. He is the author of time and eternity. He is our redeemer, our guide, our enabler, our comforter. He is Savior, brother, and friend.

These are only a few of the terms used to describe who God is. They describe who He is in Himself and who He is for His people. He is the one who reveals Himself through the Word of God, The Holy Bible. The Word and God are one.

FRUIT OF THE SPIRIT: (OUR FAITH)

"But the fruit of the Spirit is love, peace, joy, longsuffering, gentleness, meekness, goodness, faith, and temperance (self-control). Against such there is no law," (Galatians 5:22-23).

The Fruit of the Spirit is the spontaneous work of the Holy Spirit in us. The Holy Spirit produces these character traits that are found in Christ's nature. They are the byproducts of Christ's control. Without the help of the Holy Spirit, we could never obtain them. By joining our lives to Jesus, the Fruit of the Spirit will grow in us. We must love Him, know Him, remember Him, and imitate Him. As we love God and our neighbors we will fulfill the intended purpose of the law.

Because the God who sent the law also sent the Spirit, the by-products of the Spirit-filled life are in perfect harmony with the intent of God's law. A person who exhibits the Fruit of the Spirit fulfills the law far better than a person who observes the rituals, but has little love in his or her heart.

As Christians, we still have the capacity to sin, even though we have been made free from sin's power over us. We no longer have to give in to it. We have to commit our sinful tendencies to God's control daily. We have to crucify them, moment-by-moment, and draw on the Spirit's power to overcome them.

God is interested in every part of our lives, not just the spiritual part. As we live by the Holy Spirit's power, we need to submit every aspect of our lives to God; emotional, physical, social, intellectual, and vocational. Paul says this in Galatians 5:25, "Since we live by the Spirit, let us keep in step with the Spirit." The Holy Spirit is the source of your new life, so keep in step with His leading. Don't let anyone or anything determine your values and standards.

> "Trust in the Lord with all thine heart; and lean not unto thine own understanding. In all thy ways acknowledge Him, and He shall direct thy paths" (Proverbs 3:5-6).

RELEASING OUR FAITH

1. **Who is our creator?**

    ____

2. **God created the Heavens and the Earth in order to receive back the __________**
    _________________________________an_____________________________________ due him.

3. **God created the Heavens and Earth in order to provide a place where His**
    ___________________ and ___________________ for humankind might be fulfilled.

4. **Can God error or make a mistake?   Yes or No**

5. **Give 6 characteristics of God:**

    ____

    ____

    ____

    ____

    ____

    ____

6. **The Word and ____ are one.**

7. **Name the Fruit of the Spirit:**

    ____

    ____

____

____

____

____

____

____

____

____

____

____

____

8. Is there a law against walking in the Fruit of the Spirit?

Yes or No

9. Who enables us to be able to walk in the Fruit of the Spirit?

____

10. Once you are born again, do you have the capacity to sin?

Yes or No

11. Once you are born again, who is the source of your new life?

____

Chapter 4

DESCRIPTION OF THE FRUIT OF THE SPIRIT

LOVE

The Random House Dictionary of the English language defines love as the benevolent affection of God for His creatures or the reverent affection due from them to God.

1. "Though I speak with the tongues of men and of angels, and have not charity, I am become as sounding brass, or a tinkling cymbal.

2. And though I have the gift of prophecy, and understand all mysteries, and all knowledge; and though I have all faith, so that I could remove mountains, and have not charity, I am nothing.

3. And though I bestow all my goods to feed the poor, and though I give my body to be burned, and have not charity, it profiteth me nothing.

4. Charity suffereth long, and is kind; charity envieth not; Charity vaunteth not itself, is not puffed up.

5. Doth not behave itself unseemly, seeketh not her own, is not easily provoked, thinketh no evil;

6. Rejoiceth not in iniquity, but rejoiceth in the truth;

7. Beareth all things, believeth all things, hopeth all things, endureth all things.

8. Charity never faileth: but whether there be prophecies, they shall fail; whether there be tongues, they shall cease; whether there be knowledge, it shall vanish away.

9. For we know in part, and we prophesy in part.

10. But when that which is perfect is come, then that which is in part shall be done away.

11. When I was a child, I spake as a child, I understood as a child, I thought as a child: but when I became a man, I put away childish things.

12. For now we see through a glass, darkly; but then face to face: now I know in part; but then shall know even as also I am known.

13. And now abideth faith, hope, charity, these three; but the greatest of these is charity" (1 Corinthians 13:1-13).

This is the true definition of love. Love is the most important spiritual gift in the church. Love makes our gifts and actions useful. Miracle working power, great faith, and acts of dedication produce very little without love.

Our society confuses love and lust. God's love is directed outward toward others, while lust is directed inward toward ourselves. God's love is unselfish. The more we become like Christ, the more we will show love to others. We have to set aside our own desires and instincts in order to give love, while expecting nothing in return.

God gives us spiritual gifts on Earth so we can build up, serve, and strengthen fellow Christians. These spiritual gifts are for the church. In eternity, we will be made complete and perfect, and we will be in the very presence of God. The spiritual gifts will no longer be needed, so they will come to an end.

Love is the greatest of human qualities, and it is an attribute of God Himself. 1 John 4:8 says, "Whoever does not love does not know God, because God is love." Love involves unselfish service to others. It gives evidence that you care.

Faith is the foundation and content of God's message. Hope is the attitude and focus. Love is the action. When faith and hope are in line, you are free to love completely, because you understand how God loves.

"Be imitators of God, therefore, as dearly loved children and live a life of love, just as Christ loved us and gave Himself up for us as a fragrant offering and sacrifice to God" (Ephesians 5:2).

Just as we imitate our parents, we should imitate Christ. He loved us so much that He sacrificed Himself that we might live. We should show the same kind of love to others, a self-sacrificing love.

"Dear friends, let us love one another, for love comes from God. Everyone who loves has been born of God and knows God. Whoever does not love does not know God, because God is love. This is how God showed His love among us: He sent His one and only Son into the world that we might live through Him. This is love; not that we loved God, but that He loved us and sent His Son as an atoning sacrifice for our sins. Dear friends, since God so loved us, we also ought to love one another. No one has ever seen God, but if we love one another, God lives in us and His love is made complete in us.

We know that we live in Him and He in us, because He has given us His Spirit. And we have seen and testify that the Father has sent His Son to be the Savior of the world. If anyone acknowledges that Jesus is the Son of God, God lives in him and he in God. And so we know and rely on the love God has for us.

God is love. Whoever lives in love lives in God, and God in him. In this way, love is made complete among us so that we will have confidence on the day of judgment, because in this world we are like Him. There is no fear in love. But perfect love drives out fear, because fear has to do with punishment. The one who fears is not made perfect in love.

We love because He first loved us. If anyone says, 'I love God' yet hates his brother, he is a liar. For anyone who does not love his brother, whom he has seen, cannot love God, whom he has not seen. And he has given us this command: Whoever loves God must also love his brother," (1 John 4:7-21).

Everyone believes that love is important, but love is usually thought of as a feeling. In reality, love is a choice and an action as 1 Corinthians 13:4-7 shows. God is the source of our love. He loved us enough to sacrifice His Son for us. Jesus is the perfect example of love. Everything that He did in life and death was supremely loving. The Holy Spirit gives us the power to love. He lives in our hearts and makes us more and more like Christ. God's love always involves a choice and an action, and our love should be like His. How well do you display your love for God in the choices you make, and the actions you take?

John says that "God is love," not "Love is God." Our world, with its shallow and selfish view of love, has turned these words around and contaminated our understanding of love. The world thinks that love is what makes a person feel good, and that it is alright to sacrifice moral principles and others' rights in order to obtain such "love." That is not real love. It is the exact opposite-selfishness. Real love is like God, who is holy, just, and perfect. If we truly know God, we will love as He does.

It is easy to say we love God when that love doesn't cost us anything more than weekly attendance at services. But the real test of our love for God is how we treat the people right in front of us-our family members, and fellow believers. We cannot truly love God while neglecting to love those who are created in His image.

God's love is the source of all human love, and it spreads like fire. The greatest in God's Kingdom will be those who walk in the unconditional love of God, having compassion for all. It's not necessarily those who are the greatest in outward accomplishments. The love of God poured out within the believer's heart, through the Holy Spirit, is always greater than faith, hope, or anything else (Romans 5:5).

Let the LOVE OF GOD rest, rule, and abide in your hearts through the Holy Ghost. God sent His son to die for us. What more could He have done to let us know His love for us? This was the ultimate sacrifice. It is because of this sacrifice that I know He loves me. I am resting in that love.

Even though our trials may be many, we must learn to trust in God and depend on His love. Sometimes the going gets tough, but God is building a firm foundation to stand on. There is an expression that says, "I have been to rock bottom," and there is another expression that says, "God made the rock." God's grace is sufficient to take us through every trial and test.

The end results of all our experiences will only bring us closer to God. With each experience we become stronger, more refined, and as pure as gold. Consider it joy when we fall into different trials and tests, because the trying of our faith develops perseverance and stability (James 1:2).

Praise God for His LOVE and COMPASSION!!!

REVIEW ON LOVE:

1. How does The Random House Dictionary define Love?

____

____

____

____

____

____

____

2. Name four attributes of Love:

____

____

____

____

____

3. Charity (love) will fail: True or False

4. Faith, hope, and charity (love): which is the greatest?

____

5. When we give love, we should expect love in return:

True or False

6. God gives spiritual gifts on earth so we can __________________________,
    __________________________, and __________________________
    fellow Christians.

7. What is the greatest human quality? __________________________

8. God does not just love us, but God is __________________________.

9. __________________________ is the foundation and content of God's
    message; hope is the attitude and focus; __________________________ is the action.

10. Just as we imitate our parents, we should also imitate

    ____

11. Where does Love come from? __________________________

12. Are we a liar if we say we love God and hate our brother?

                        Yes or No

13. Love is not a feeling, it is a __________________________.

14. James 1:2 says, "Consider it joy when we fall into different trials and tests,
    because the trying of our faith builds or develops
    __________________________ and __________________________."

15. Are there any bad consequences to LOVE?

                        Yes or No

PEACE

The Revell Bible Dictionary defines peace as wholeness, unity, harmony, prosperity, health, and fulfillment. Theologically, inner harmony and harmonious interpersonal relationships with others made possible by a personal relationship with God. Peace in Hebrew is Shalom.

Peace denotes far more than the absence of war and conflict. The basic meaning of shalom is harmony, wholeness, soundness, well-being, and success in all areas of life.

- It can refer to tranquility in international relationships, such as peace between warring nations (1 Kings 4:24).

- It can be experienced as a settled feeling within a nation during times of prosperity and no civil war (2 Samuel 3:21-23).

- Peace can be seen as wholeness and harmony in human relationships, both inside the home (1 Corinthians 7:15) and outside the home (Romans 12:18).

- Peace can refer to one's personal sense of wholeness and well-being, being free from anxiety, and at peace within our own souls (Psalm 4:8) and with God (Romans 5:1).

- Shalom describes the original created world that existed in perfect harmony and wholeness (Genesis 1:2).

When God created the Heavens and the Earth, He created a world of peace. The total well-being of creation is reflected in the summary statement, after God had finished creating the world, "Everything was very good" (Genesis 1:31).

Although Satan initiated the destruction of peace in the world in the garden of Eden, God had planned to restore Shalom. At Jesus' birth, the angels proclaimed that God's peace had now come to the Earth (Luke 2:14). Jesus Himself came to destroy the works of the devil (1 John 3:8) and to break down all barriers of conflict that are a part of our lives, thus making peace (Ephesians 2:12-17). Jesus gave His disciples His peace as a lasting legacy, before He went to the cross (John 14:27). By His death and resurrection, Jesus disarmed the hostile principalities and powers, and made peace possible (Colossians 1:20; 2:14-15).

Therefore, when we believe in Jesus Christ, we are justified by faith and have peace with God (Romans 5:1). We have reconciled with Him. There is no more hostility between us, no sin blocking our relationship with Him. Peace with God is possible because He paid the price for our sins, through His death on the cross.

The message that Christians proclaimed is the good news of peace. We may never avoid strife in the world around us, but in God we can know perfect peace, even in turmoil. When we are devoted to Him, our whole attitude is steady and stable. Supported by God's unchanging love and mighty power, we are not shaken by the surrounding chaos. "You will keep him in perfect peace, whose mind is stayed on thee" (Isaiah 26:3).

Through the course of our lives, there will be many storms. Without the peace of God, some of our storms can be unbearable.

But the peace of God, will transcend all understanding, and will guard your hearts and your minds in Christ Jesus" (Philippians 4:7). His peace will give you the feeling of total inner tranquility.

To experience this peace as part of our lives, we must be united with Christ in active faith. The first step is to believe in the Lord Jesus Christ. When we do that we are justified by faith (Romans 3:21-28), and have peace with God (Romans 5:1).

To know God's peace, He has given us the Holy Spirit, who works His fruit in us-one aspect of which is peace (Galatians 5:22). With the Spirit's help, we must pray for peace (Jeremiah 29:7), let peace rule in our hearts (Colossians 3:15), seek peace, and pursue it (2 Timothy 2:22), and do our best to live in peace with others (Romans 12:18).

The Biblical concept of "peace" is total and profound. It touches on our relationship with God, with our inner self, with other believers, and with the world at large. Biblically, peace is no mere absence of strife, but the active experience of a harmony that promotes total well-being. Peace is always the product of God's active involvement in our lives, and God's intervention is essential. This is because sin has so marred individuals and society, that strife is our constant companion. Only God's saving work can bring us an experience of His peace.

When we call on God from hearts that sincerely endeavor to abide in His Word (John 15:7), then the peace of God will flood our troubled souls. When we lay our troubles before God in prayer, the peace of God will stand guard at the door of our hearts and minds, preventing the cares of life and the heartaches of disappointment from overthrowing our lives and hope in Christ (Romans 8:35-39).

"Peace" is another fruit of the spirit and against peace there is no law.

PEACE REVIEW

1. **Define peace:**

____

____

____

____

____

____

____

2. **Who initiated the destruction of peace in the world?**

____

3. **Jesus came to ________________________________ the works of the devil.**

4. **God's peace will give you the feeling of total inner tranquility:**

True or False

5. **Who works in us to give us peace?**

____

____

6. **Are there any bad consequences or laws against peace?**

Yes or No

7. **What does peace mean to you or how has it brought you through some of the storms in your life? (15 lines)**

____

____

____

____

____

JOY

The Revell Bible Dictionary, in the Old Testament defines Joy as a sense of exultation rooted in God and God's acts for His people, which typically is expressed in exuberant public worship. In the New Testament, Joy is an inner sense of exultation and confidence in God, which the Holy Spirit works in the lives of believers and which we experience despite present sufferings.

Joy is an integral part of our salvation in Christ. It is an inner peace and delight in God the Father, Son, and Holy Spirit, and in the blessing that flows from our relationship with them (2 Corinthians 13:14). Scriptural teaching about joy includes the following:

(1) Joy is associated with the salvation God provides in Christ

(2) (1 Peter 1:3) and with God's Word (Jeremiah 15:16).

Joy flows from God as a gift of the Spirit (Romans 15:13). It does not come to us automatically, but is experienced only as we maintain in an abiding relationship with Christ (John 15:1-11). Our joy becomes greater when the Holy Spirit mediates a deep sense of the presence and nearness of God in our lives (John 14:15-21). Jesus taught that the fullness of joy is inseparably connected to our abiding in His word, loving others, obeying His commandments (John 15:7, 10-11), and being separated from the world (John 17:13-17).

(3) Be joyful as a delight in God's nearness and His redemptive gifts cannot be destroyed by pain, suffering weakness, or difficult circumstances (Matthew 5:12).

Scripture usually sets joy apart from mere happiness. Even the joy of Old Testament saints, in material blessings, is rooted not in the things themselves but in the evidence they provide of God's covenant love. In the New Testament, joy often wells up in the most painful and desperate situations.

Such joy, known by those who are obedient to Jesus, is supernaturally produced as we look ahead with confidence, to reaffirm our faith in the goodness and ultimate triumph of our God.

Matthew 15:9-11, as Jesus is teaching His disciples about the vine and the branches says, "As the Father has loved me, so have I loved you. Now remain in my love. If you obey my commands, you will remain in my love, just as I have obeyed my

Father's commands and remain in His love. I have told you this so that my joy may be in you and that your joy may be complete."

We can feel good when things are going well, but when hardships come, we sink into depression. True joy transcends beyond the moving waves of circumstance. Joy comes from a consistent relationship with Jesus Christ. When our lives are intertwined with His, He will help us walk through adversity without sinking into enervating lows, and manage prosperity without moving into deceptive highs. The joy of living with Jesus Christ daily will keep us level-headed, no matter how high or how low our circumstances.

> "Consider it pure joy, my brothers, whenever you face trials of many kinds, because you know that the testing of your faith develops perseverance. Perseverance must finish its work so that you may be mature and complete, not lacking anything" (James 1:2).

James doesn't say if you face trials, but whenever you face them. He assumes that we will have trials, and that it is possible to profit from them. James tells us to turn our hardships into times of learning. Tough times can teach us perseverance which is patience and steadfastness.

David is rejoicing in God's protection and peace in Psalm 4. We can place our confidence in God because He will listen when we call on Him. In Psalm 4:6-7 David says, "Let the light of your face shine upon us, O Lord. You have filled my heart with greater joy." Here, David's heart was glad because he had found the secret to joy. True joy is far deeper than happiness. We can feel joy in spite of our deepest troubles. Happiness is temporary, because it is based on external circumstances, but joy is lasting, because it is based on God's presence within us.

The joy of the Lord is our strength (Nehemiah 8:10). Declaring God's Word and a sincere desire to follow its instructions will result in a true, heartfelt joy. "The joy of the Lord" is based on reconciliation with God and the presence of the Spirit in our lives. This is maintained by the assurance that we have been forgiven in Christ, restored to fellowship with God, and we now live in harmony with His will. This joy is like a fortress to guard us from the troubles and temptations of each day (Galatians 5:22) and has the power and motivation to persevere in faith until the end.

As we contemplate His daily presence, we will find contentment. As we understand the future that He has for us, we will experience joy. Don't base your life on circumstances, but on GOD.

In life you will encounter trials and tests (dark places) that you have no idea how to get out of. Worry and oppression can take a hold of your mind. But what does the Word of God say? It says, "Count it all joy when you fall into divers temptations; Knowing this, that the trying of your faith worketh patience" (James 1:2-3). Your adversary will convince you that you need to give up, because you cannot win. The joy of the Lord will give you the strength that you need to stay in the race. As you persevere God will assure you that the race is neither given to the swift nor to the strong, but to those who endure until the end. You hear His voice saying, "Be steadfast and immovable, because the victory has already been won." Knowing these things through a personal relationship with God will win the battle every time.

REVIEW ON JOY

1. **Define Joy:**

____

____

____

____

____

2. **Joy is an integral part of our** _________________________________ **in Christ.**

3. **Joy flows from** _________________________________ **as a gift of the Spirit.**

4. **Scripture set Joy apart from mere** _________________________________.

5. _________________________________ **transcends beyond the moving waves of circumstance.**

6. **Joy comes from a consistent relationship with** _________________________________
   _________________________________.

7. **The testing of your Faith develops** _________________________________.

8. **Will everyone experience trials in this life?** **Yes or No**

9. **Joy lasts because it is based on** _________________________________ **presence within us.**

10. **The** _________________________________ **of the Lord is our strength.**

11. **Don't base your life on circumstances, but on** _________________________________.

LONGSUFFERING (PATIENCE)

The Revell Bible Dictionary defines longsuffering as a quality of patience displayed in God's willingness to delay punishment in order to give human beings the opportunity to repent. In the Old Testament longsuffering is demonstrated in God's slowness to anger, as in Psalm 86:15. In the New Testament, long-suffering is displayed in God's tolerance and patience, and kindness that moves Him to give men occasion to repent.

> "The Lord is not slow in keeping His promise, as some understand slowness. He is patient with us, not wanting anyone to perish, but everyone to come to repentance" (2 Peter 3:9, Life Application Bible).

God is not on our timetable. A thousand years is like one day to God. He seemed slow to those believers who were being persecuted in Peter's day. Scoffers (unbelievers who mocked and ridiculed believers) would say that Jesus was never coming back. Peter refuted their argument by explaining God's mastery over time. We must do the work in which God has called us, and believe that He will return as He promised.

Unbelievers are still mocking God's people today. Jesus is giving them more time to repent and turn to Him. We should live with the realization that time is short, and that we have important work to do.

Patience in Greek is the capacity to remain self-controlled, despite difficult circumstances or actions by others that might be expected to cause anger.

God displays "kindness, tolerance, and patience" by withholding punishment. Patience is given priority in Paul's classic description of Christian Love (1 Corinthians 13:4) and is commended in no less than twelve of the New Testament Epistles. Taken together, New Testament references show that patience is a basic Christian attitude to be practiced in our relationships with others, and exercised in difficult situations.

Longsuffering is a quality that God first expressed in the Garden of Eden, after Adam and Eve's sin, when he did not destroy the human race as He had a right to do (Genesis 2:16-17). God was also patient in the days of Noah, while the Ark was being built (1 Peter 3:20). God is still longsuffering, with the sinful human race. He does not presently judge to destroy the world, because He is patiently giving everyone an opportunity to repent and be saved (2 Peter 3:9).

"Be completely humble and gentle; be patient, bearing with one another in Love" (Ephesians 4:2). No one will ever be perfect here on Earth, so we must accept and love other Christians, in spite of their faults.

When we see faults in fellow believers, we should be patient and gentle in dealing with them. Is there someone whose actions or personality really annoys you? Rather than dwelling on that person's weakness or looking for faults, pray for him/her. Then do even more. Spend time together and see if you can learn to like him/her. When you get to know people, you tend to see them in a totally different light.

Sometimes, we may find ourselves angry at others' sin. Even though we need to speak out against sin, we have to be very careful in how we do so. We should do so in a spirit of humility.

> "Therefore thou art inexcusable, O man, whosoever thou art that judgest: for wherein thou judgest another, thou condemnest thyself; for thou that judgest doest the same things. But we are sure that the judgment of God is according to truth against them which commit such things. And thinketh thou this, O man, that judgest them which do such things, and doest the same, that thou shalt escape the judgment of God? Or despisest thou the riches of His goodness and forbearance and longsuffering; not knowing that the goodness of God leadeth thee to repentance" (Roman 2:1-4)?

Often, the sins we notice most clearly in others, are the ones that have taken root in us. If we look closely at ourselves, we may find that we are committing the same sins in more socially acceptable forms. For instance, a person who gossips may be very critical of others who gossip about him/her.

When Paul read his letters in the Roman Church, it is no doubt that many heads nodded as he condemned idol worshipers, homosexual practices, and violent people. But what really surprised his listeners is when he turned on them and said in effect, "You have no excuses. You are just as bad!" Paul was stressing the fact that nobody is good enough to save himself or herself.

If we want to avoid punishment and live eternally with Christ, all of us, whether we have been murderers and molesters or whether we have been honest, hard-working, solid citizens, we must depend totally on God's grace. Paul is not discussing whether some sins are worse than others. Any sin is enough to lead us to depend on Jesus Christ for salvation and eternal life. We have all sinned repeatedly, and there is no way apart from Christ to be saved from sin's consequences.

In all kindness, God holds back His judgment (longsuffering), giving people time to repent. It is easy to mistake God's patience for approval of the wrong way we are living. Self-evaluation is difficult, and it is even more difficult to expose our conduct to God and let him tell us where we need to change. As Christians, or Kingdom Citizens, we must pray constantly that God will point out our sins so that He can heal them. Unfortunately, we are more likely to be amazed at God's patience with others than humbled at His patience with us.

Be patient and kind to others. Use wisdom and understanding and don't be so easy to give up and throw in the towel. Pray for people and ask God for guidance. We may not be able to handle every problem that we are confronted with. Some problems may have to be referred to another counselor. Trust God. He will guide you.

There is no limit on how long it may take to solve a problem. "Let us not be weary in well doing: for in due season we shall reap, if we faint not" (Galatians 6:9).

Practice patience (longsuffering). That is the key. Time is not the issue. Cast your cares on God and let Him handle the problem.

"Thank God for Jesus!!!!"

LONGSUFFERING (PATIENCE) REVIEW

1. Longsuffering is the same thing as ________________________________.

2. God is patient with us because He does not want anyone to

   ____

3. God and man are on the same timetable:

   True or False

4. One thousand years is like a ______________________________ to God.

5. Unbelievers who mocked and ridiculed believers are called

   ____

6. Are unbelievers still mocking God's people today?

   Yes or No

7. Patience in Greek is the capacity to remain ____________________.

8. ____ is a basic Christian
   attitude that should be practiced in our relationships with others.

9. When did God first display how patient He really was?

   ____

10. Paul stressed that no one is good enough to save himself or herself. We all need a savior.

True or False

11. Don't waste your time with someone who does not want to be saved.

True or False

GENTLENESS

The **Random House Dictionary** defines gentleness as being kind or amiable; mild, not severe, rough or violent; moderate, thoughtful, calm, considerate. Yielding, soothing.

Gentleness is perhaps best understood by its opposites. A gentle person does not selfishly insist on his own way. A gentle person is not easy to anger, or arrogant. They are not rigid and do not demand their rights or strict justice, but makes allowances for others. The calm, reasonable, caring, spirit associated with gentleness is a mark of inner beauty and is, "Of great worth in God's eyesight" (1 Peter 3:4).

God desires that we (Christians) have a spirit of modesty. God highly values and exalts our gentle and quiet disposition (Matthew 11:29). He desires us to be meek, gentle, and unassuming with a gracious submissiveness and a genuine concern for others (Galatians 5:23). He wants us to possess a quiet spirit that is not boisterous, and does not create disturbances. Never slander anyone. Humbly be at peace with all men, and be considerate of them.

Jesus Himself is described as a gentle person (2 Corinthians 10:1), and Christian leaders are required to cultivate this attribute (Titus 3:2). Christians also have obligations toward all fellow citizens outside the church, and by their gentle dispositions may influence them for good. Gentleness is produced in the human personality by the Holy Spirit, (Galatians 5:22-23).

"And the servant of the Lord must not strive, but be gentle unto all men, apt to teach, patient" (2 Timothy 2:24). As a teacher, Timothy helped those who were confused about the truth. Paul's advice to Timothy, and to all who teach God's truth, is to be kind and gentle, patiently, and courteously explaining the truth. Good teaching never promotes quarrels or foolish arguments.

Whether you are teaching school, leading a Bible study, or preaching in church, remember to listen to people's questions and treat them respectfully, while avoiding foolish debates. If you do this, those who oppose you will be more willing to hear what you have to say, and perhaps turn from their error.

GENTLENESS REVIEW

1. Gentleness is being _________________________________ and _____________
____.

2. A gentle person insists on his own way: True or False

3. A gentle person is not easy to get _______________________ or arrogant.

4. A gentle person makes allowances for others: True or False

5. God wants us to have a _________________________________ of modesty.

6. Humbly be at _________________________________ with all men and be
considerate to them.

7. Jesus Himself is described as a ___________________ person.

8. Gentleness is produced in the human personality by the _________________
_____________________________________.

9. Good teaching never promotes _________________________ and ____
____.

MEEKNESS

The Merriam Webster Dictionary defines meekness as, the quality or state of being meek; a mild, moderate, humble, or submissive quality. The quality of having a patient and gentle attitude. The King James version of the Old Testament often translates meek in Hebrew, as 'anawah' ("suffering," "oppressed," and thus "humble"). But this is not quite the same as the New Testament concept.

In the New Testament, meekness is the opposite of arrogance. It suggests dependence on God in a gentle, non-threatening demeanor toward others. Far from being weak, meekness requires great inner strength, both in faith and self-control.

Being meek is being humble. The Christian virtue of humility affects relationships with others, as well as reflects personal dependence on God. The humble, meek person is not concerned with his prestige.

"Do nothing out of selfish ambition or vain conceit, but in humility consider others better than yourselves. Each of us should look not only to our own interests, but also to the interests of others" (Philippians 2:3-4). Having freedom from a sense of one's own importance, with honest concern for others and personal dependence on God, is a perfect concept of humility. This makes being humbled one of the most mentioned and encouraged of Christian virtues.

Often, we worry about our position and status hoping to get proper recognition for what we do. Peter advises us to remember that God's recognition counts more than human praise. God is able and willing to bless us in His timing. Humbly obey God, regardless of present circumstances and in due season, He will lift you up.

"Young men, in the same way, are submissive to those who are older. All of you, clothe yourselves with humility toward one another, because, "God opposes the proud but gives grace to the humble" (1 Peter 5:5).

These were Peter's instructions. Both old and young can benefit from these instructions. Pride often keeps older people from trying to understand young people, and keeps young people from listening to older people. Peter told both old and young people to be humble, and to serve each other. Young men should follow the leadership of older men, who should lead by example. Respect those who are older than you, listen to those younger than you, and be humble enough to admit that you can learn from each other.

One of the greatest examples of meekness or humility is as Philippians 2:7-8 says, "Jesus made Himself of no reputation and took upon Him the form of a servant, and was made in the likeness of men: and being found in fashion as a man, He humbled Himself, and became obedient unto death, even the death on the cross."

Death on a cross (crucifixion) was the form of capital punishment that Romans used for notorious criminals. It is excruciatingly painful and humiliating. Prisoners were nailed or tied to a cross and left to die. Death might not come for several days, and it usually came by suffocation when the weight of the weakened body made breathing more and more difficult. Jesus died as one who was cursed (Galatians 3:13). How amazing that the perfect man would die this most shameful death, so that we would not have to face eternal punishment! Thank God for Jesus. He did it for us. What a mighty God we serve. He humbled Himself as unto death that we would have eternal life. The least we can do is to be obedient to His Word.

MEEKNESS REVIEW

1. Define Meekness:

____

____

____

____

____

____

____

**2. The Hebrew word for meekness is _______________________________,
Old Testament.**

3. In the New Testament Meekness is the opposite of

____

**4. Meekness requires great inner strength, both in _______________
and self-control.**

5. Being meek is being _______________________________.

6. The humble, meek person is concerned about his prestige.

True or False

**7. Do nothing out of selfish ambition or vain conceit, but in humility consider
others better than _______________________ (Philippians 2:3).**

8. **We often worry about our position and status, hoping to get proper recognition for what we do.**

True or False

9. **God opposes the proud but gives grace to the _______________, (1 Peter 5:5).**

10. **What keeps older people from trying to understand younger people and keeps young people from listening to older People? ____.**

11. **What is one of the greatest examples of meekness or humility in the Bible?**

____

____

____

____

____

____

____

____

____

____

____

____

GOODNESS

The Random House Dictionary defines Goodness as the state or quality of being good. Moral excellence; virtue. Kindness, generosity, excellence of quality.

Original creation, a beautiful woman, a fertile field, an attractive child, the married state, are all described in scripture as "good."

In an absolute moral sense, only God is truly good. Goodness is a divine attribute (Psalm 25:9), which is expressed in God's relationship with Israel (Psalm 73:1), and with all mankind (Psalm 145:9). James insists that God neither tempts nor is tempted by evil but that "Every good and perfect gift is from above, coming down from the Father of the heavenly lights, who does not change" (James 1:17).

To speak of something or someone being "good" begs evaluation. On a human level, some people are more moral than others. Jesus Himself noted that we, though evil, "Know how to give good gifts to (our) children" (Matthew 7:11). But when the standard of comparison is God, "There is no one who does good, not even one" (Romans 3:12).

God, who is good in an absolute moral sense, has revealed "what is good" to humankind. Micah sums goodness up as, "To act justly and to love mercy and to walk humbly with your God." God's commandments are good and mark out a pathway which is morally right. They are also attractive and beneficial, for doing good, keep us from harm, and guide us to our benefit.

Both Testaments call on God's covenant people to "trust in the Lord and do good" (Psalm 37:3). The New Testament lays great stress on doing good. Believers are, "To do good, to be rich in good deeds, to be generous and willing to share" (1 Timothy 6:18).

> "Charge them that are rich in this world, that they be not high-minded, nor trust in uncertain riches, but in the living God, who giveth us richly all things to enjoy; That they do good, that they be rich in good works, ready to distribute, willing to communicate; Laying up in store for themselves a good foundation against the time to come, that they may lay hold on eternal life" (1 Timothy 6:17-19).

Ephesus was a very wealthy city, and the Ephesian Church had many wealthy members. Paul's advice to Timothy was to deal with any potential problems, by teaching that having riches carries great responsibility. Those who have money must be generous, but not arrogant just because they have a lot to give. They must be careful not to use money as their security, but instead put their hope in the living God. We may not have material wealth, but we can still be rich in good deeds. No matter how poor we may be, we still have something to share with someone.

Good works are not the way people can earn salvation, but they are a product of salvation. Salvation is "not by work, so that no one can boast." Yet God's salvation so renews human beings that they become "God's workmanship, created in Christ Jesus to do good works, which God prepared in advance for us to do" (Ephesians 2:9-10).

> "Let us not become weary in doing good, for at the proper time we will reap a harvest if we do not give up. Therefore, as we have opportunity, let us do good to all people, especially to those who belong to the family of believers" (Galatians 6:9-10).

Sometimes it is discouraging to continue doing right, because our deeds go unnoticed or we see no tangible results. But Paul challenged the Galatians, and God challenges us to keep on doing good and to trust Him for the results. In due time, we will reap a harvest of blessing.

We are God's workmanship (work of art, masterpiece). Our salvation comes only from God. It is His powerful, creative work in us. If God considers us His works of art, we dare not treat ourselves or others with disrespect or as inferior work. God's intention is that our salvation will result in (good) acts of service. We are not saved merely for our own benefit, but to serve Christ and build up the church (Ephesians 4:12).

GOODNESS REVIEW

1. **The Random House Dictionary defines Goodness as:**

____

____

____

____

____

____

2. **In an absolute moral sense, only _____________________________ is truly good.**

3. **Every good and perfect gift is from above: True or False**

4. **There is no one who does good, not even one person, when the comparison is**
____.

5. **Both testaments call on God's covenant people to _________________________ in the Lord and do good (Psalm 37:3).**

6. **_______________________________________ was a very wealthy city, and the Ephesian church probably had many wealthy members.**

7. **Be careful not to use money as your _______________________________.**

8. **Instead of trusting money you should trust ____________________________.**

9. **We are God's ____.**

FAITH

The Random House Dictionary defines faith as, confidence or trust in a person or thing. Belief that is not based on proof. Belief in God. The obligation or loyalty or fidelity to a person, promise engagement, etc.

The King James version of the bible defines faith as, "The substance of things hoped for, the evidence of things not seen" (Hebrews 11:1).

In the Bible, faith is a life-shaping attitude toward God. The person with faith considers God's revelation of Himself, and of truth, to be certain and sure. The person with faith then responds to God with trust, love, and obedience.

God made promises to Abraham, and the Bible says, "Abraham believed the Lord, and He (God) credited him as righteousness" (Genesis 15:6). In the New Testament, the object of faith is Jesus. Only twelve times does the New Testament speak of "faith in God" rather than faith in the Lord Jesus Christ, because Jesus is now the one in whom God has fully expressed Himself.

Biblical faith has two aspects. On God's part, there is an act of revelation that calls for a response. On man's part there is a response of faith that evaluates God's revelation as trustworthy and responds wholeheartedly to the Lord.

Thus, God presents Jesus as His son, whose death wins us forgiveness, and we by faith rely completely on Jesus for our salvation.

The best way to understand faith is to look at significant New Testament passages describing it. Here are some Biblical examples of Faith (The Revell Bible Dictionary):

Look at Romans Chapter 4. This chapter looks back to Genesis, focusing on Abraham's response to God's promise of a child. Abraham believed God's promise of a child long before he saw signs of his wife's pregnancy. In Romans 4:18-21 it says, "Against all hope, Abraham in hope believed and so became the father of many nations, just as it had been said to him, 'So shall your offspring be.' Without weakening in his faith, he faced the fact that his body was as good as dead since he was about a hundred years old, and that Sarah's womb was also dead. Yet he did not waver through unbelief regarding the promise of God, but was strengthened in his faith and gave glory to God, being fully persuaded that God had the power to do what He had promised."

Abraham's faith was in God Himself and in God's power to do what He promised. He never doubted God. His faith was strengthened by the obstacles he faced, and his life was an example of faith in action. Also, we who believe in Jesus must have confidence. We may not understand the how or why, but we must be fully persuaded that God can do for us what He has promised.

In Hebrews 11, this great chapter begins, "Faith is being sure of what we hope for and certain of what we do not see." The chapter continues by listing men and women whose faith in God was expressed by actions. Noah built an ark long before he saw the rains that God warned would flood the earth.

In each case, faith shaped the believer's perception of the future and made a difference in the choices that they made. Faith is sure and it is certain. The beginning point of faith is believing in God's character (He is who He says). The end point is believing in God's promises (He will do what He says). When we believe that God will fulfill His promises, even though we don't see them materializing yet, we demonstrate true faith.

Faith should shape our perspective, too, transforming the way we live our lives. We who believe in Jesus can be sure of what we hope for, even though we cannot yet see it.

In James 2 we understand that "Faith" can be ineffectual in at least two ways. A person who places his confidence in false or empty objects is invalid. Or a person can "believe" intellectually, without a personal commitment to what is believed. In this case, faith's response is inadequate.

James illustrates this second problem with the observation that demons even believe that God exists. A "faith" that exists simply as an agreement that something is true, without that wholehearted response which motivates action is a futile faith. The faith in God to which we are called in Jesus engages our total response to the Lord. We consider God trustworthy, and because of our belief, everything we think and do is shaped by that conviction.

Faith cometh by hearing and hearing by the Word of God (Romans 10:17). The more Word you know and understand, the more faith you have. Understanding and believing the Word of God is the key to faith. This is the reason why God says in His

Word (Matthew 6:33), "But seek first His Kingdom and His righteousness, and all these things will be given to you as well." This means to turn to God for help first, to fill your thoughts with His desires, to take His character for your pattern, and to serve and obey Him in everything. This is done by studying His Word, so we will know what and how to do His will. His will is His Word (faith).

Faith, biblically understood, has life-transforming effects. When we place our faith in Jesus, the Bible affirms that we have "eternal life, and we will not be condemned," but have "crossed over from death to life" (John 5:24). This faith expresses itself presently in a love for God and for others. The Holy Spirit produces love, joy, peace, patience, kindness, goodness, faithfulness, gentleness, and self-control (Galatians 5:1-23).

FAITH REVIEW

1. **How does the Random House Dictionary define Faith?**

____

____

____

____

____

2. **The King James version of the bible, Hebrews 11:1 defines "faith" as:**

____

____

____

____

____

____

____

3. **In the Bible, _______________________________________**
    is a life-shaping attitude toward God.

4. **When Abraham believed God, it was credited to him as**

____

(Gen. 15:6).

5. **Abraham's _________________________________ was in God and that God**
    would do what he promised.

6. **Did Noah have Faith in God (when he built the Ark)?**

Yes or No

7. **Faith is sure and it is certain:**   **True or False**

8. **Even demons believe God exists:**   **True or False**

9. **Faith comes by** ____ **and hearing by the Word of God.**

10. **God's will is His** ____.

TEMPERANCE–SELF CONTROL

The Revell Bible Dictionary defines temperance as, power over one's own actions; moderation; good sense. In the New Testament, self-control, especially mastery of one's passions, is viewed as one of the virtues that flows from a relationship with Christ. This is mediated by the indwelling Holy Spirit.

"A man who controls his temper is better than one who takes a city" (Proverbs 16:32). Unless a person is able to control himself, power over others is meaningless.

Success in business, school, or home life can be destroyed by a person who has lost control of his temper. It is a great personal victory to control your temper. When you feel yourself ready to explode, remember that losing control may cause you to forfeit what you want the most.

In the New Testament (Titus 2:2-5) self-control, especially mastery of one's passions, is viewed as one of the virtues that flows from a relationship with Christ. This is mediated by the indwelling Holy Spirit.

In this passage, Paul was teaching what must be taught to various groups. Self-control was a very important aspect of early Christianity. The Christian community consisted of people from many different backgrounds and viewpoints, making conflict inevitable. The Christians lived in pagan and hostile environments. To stay above reproach, they had to have wisdom and discernment to be discreet, and to master their wills, tongues, and passions so that Christ would not be dishonored.

Solomon is giving words of wisdom to his leaders. He says, "Like a city whose walls are broken down is a man who lacks self-control" (Proverbs 25:28). Even though city walls restricted the inhabitants' movements, people were happy to have them. Without walls, they would have been vulnerable to attack by any passing group of marauders (people who robbed for goods or valuables). Self-control limits us, but it is necessary. An out-of-control life is subject to all kinds of enemy attacks. Self-control is like a wall for defense and protection.

> **"For the grace of God that brings salvation has appeared to all men. It teaches us to say 'no' to ungodliness and worldly passions, and to live self-controlled, upright and godly lives in this present age, while we wait for the blessed hope, the glorious appearing of our great God and Savior, Jesus Christ, who gave himself for us to redeem us from**

all wickedness and to purify for Himself a people that are his very own, eager to do what is good" (Titus 2:11-14).

The power to live as a Christian comes from the Holy Spirit. Because Christ died and rescued us from sin, we are free from sin's control. God gives us the power and understanding to live according to His will and to do good. Then we can look for Christ's wonderful return with eager expectation and hope. It is not enough to renounce sin and evil desires. We must also live actively for God. To fight against lust, we must say "no" to temptation, but we must also say "yes" to active service for Christ.

Therefore, prepare your minds for action. Be self-controlled. Set your hope fully on the grace to be given to you when Jesus Christ is revealed (1 Peter 1:13). The imminent return of Christ should motivate us to live for Him. This means being mentally alert, disciplined, and focused.

The end of all things is near. Therefore, be clear minded and self-controlled so that you can pray, (1 Peter 4:7). It is important to pray regularly, and it is also important to reach out to needy people. Your possessions, status, and power will mean nothing in God's Kingdom, but you will spend eternity with other people. Invest your time and talents where they will make an eternal difference.

Your enemy, the devil, prowls around like a roaring lion looking for someone to devour (1 Peter 5:8). Lions attack sick, young, or straggling animals. They choose victims who are alone, or not alert. Watch out for Satan when suffering or being persecuted. People can be so focused on their problems that they become vulnerable to his attacks. Keep your eyes on Christ and resist the devil and he will flee (James 4:7).

Praise God for His Grace, His Grace is sufficient!!!!

TEMPERANCE-SELF CONTROL REVIEW

1. **What is Temperance?**

____

____

____

____

____

____

2. **"A man who controls his _________________________ is better than one who takes a city" (Proverbs 16: 32).**

3. **It is a great personal victory to _________________________ your temper.**

4. **_________________________ is one of the virtues that flows from a relationship with Christ.**

5. **It is not necessary to have self-control: True or False**

6. **Self-control is like a wall of _________________________ and _________________________.**

7. **The power to live as a Christian (Christ-like) comes from the _________________________.**

8. **Your enemy, the _________________________ prowls around like a roaring lion, looking for someone to devour.**

9. **Keep your eyes on _________________________ and resist the devil, and he will flee (James 4:7).**

COMMENTS ON THE FRUIT OF THE SPIRIT

There are no restrictions when it involves a lifestyle indicated here known as the "Fruit of the Spirit." This is the lifestyle that God planned for us, from the beginning. There is no law against the things of the Spirit. Christians can, and ought, to practice these virtues repeatedly. They will never discover a law that prohibits us from living according to these principles.

The Fruit of the Spirit is the spontaneous work of the Holy Spirit in us. The Spirit produces these character traits that are found in the nature of Christ. These are the by-products of Christ's control. We cannot obtain them on our own. We must have His help. If we want the Fruit of the Spirit to grow in us, we must join our lives to His (John 15:4-5). We must know Him, love Him, and imitate Him. Then we will fulfill the intended purpose of the law-to love God and our neighbors.

> "Live by the Spirit, and you will not gratify the desires of the sinful nature. For the sinful nature desires what is contrary to the Spirit, and the Spirit what is contrary to the sinful nature. They are in conflict with each other so that you do not do what you want. But if you are led by the Spirit, you are not under the law" (Galatians 5: 16-18).

The Holy Spirit and the sinful nature are two forces within us, which are in conflict with one another. Even though the Holy Spirit is the stronger force, if we rely on our own wisdom, we will make bad choices. If we try to follow the spirit by our own human effort, we will fail. The only way to freedom, from our evil desires, is through the empowerment of the Holy Spirit.

If your desire is to have the qualities of the Holy Spirit present in your life, then you know that you are being led by the Spirit. Being led by the Holy Spirit involves the desire to hear, the readiness to obey God's Word, and the sensitivity to discern between your feelings and His promptings. Live each day guided by the Holy Spirit. Then the words of Christ will be in your mind, the love of Christ will be behind your actions, and the power of Christ will help you control your selfish desires.

COMMENTS ON THE FRUIT
OF THE SPIRIT REVIEW

1. **Are there any restrictions when it comes to the Fruit of the Spirit?**
    Yes or No

2. **There will never be a law that prohibits us from living according to the Fruit of the Spirit:**
    True or False

3. **Can we obtain the Fruit of the Spirit on our own?**
    Yes or No

4. **We must have the help of the _______________________ in order to live by the Spirit.**

5. **If we are led by the Spirit, we will not gratify the desires of the Sinful Nature (Galatians 5:16).**
    True or False

6. **Name the two forces that are within us that are in conflict with one another?**

    ____

    ____

7. **The only way to freedom from our evil desires is through the empowering of the _______________________________________.**

8. **Live each day guided by the Holy Spirit:**
    True or False

DIFFERENT CLASSES OF PEOPLE

"But the natural man receiveth not the things of the Spirit of God: for they are foolishness unto him: neither can he know them, because they are spiritually discerned. But he that is spiritual judgeth all things, yet he himself is judged of no man"(1 Corinthians 2: 14-15).

Scripture normally divides all humans into two classes. (1) The natural man, and (2) the spiritual man. Not all Christians put forth the necessary effort to fully overcome their sinful nature. Paul notes in (1 Corinthians 3:1, 3) that some of the Corinthian Christians were behaving in a carnal or fleshly way. Paul called the Corinthians infants in the Christian life, as they were not yet spiritually healthy and mature. They were acting like children, allowing divisions to distract them. Immature Christians are "worldly," being controlled by their own desires. This brings us to a third class of people, (3) The Carnal Christian. Let's look at the first class:

(1) The Natural Man: But the natural, non-spiritual man does not accept, welcome, or admit into his heart the gifts and teachings, revelations of the Spirit of God. They are folly (meaningless nonsense) to him, and he is incapable of knowing them–of progressively recognizing, understanding and becoming better acquainted with them–because they are spiritually discerned and estimated and appreciated (1 Corinthians 2:14, Amp. Bible).

This is the unregenerate or fleshly person, one who is governed by mere natural instincts. This person does not have the Holy Spirit (Romans 8:9), is under the dominion of Satan (Acts 26:18), and is enslaved to the body and its passions (Ephesians 2:3). This person belongs to, and sympathizes with the world. They reject the righteous

ways of the Spirit. The natural person cannot understand God and His ways, but instead relies totally on human reasoning and emotions.

They cannot grasp the fact that God's Spirit lives inside of the believer. Unbelievers will not understand or approve of the decision to follow Christ. They reject God and cannot hear His message. The belief about God seems silly to them. The lines of communication are broken, and they cannot hear what God is saying to them. Without the guidance of the Holy Spirit, we cannot comprehend God (Romans 11:34).

(2) The Spiritual man (1 Corinthians 2:15) states, "But the Spiritual man tries all things–(that is) he examines, investigates, inquires into, questions, and discerns all things; but is not to be put on trial and judged by no one. He can read the meaning of everything, but no one can properly discern or appraise or get an insight into him."

The Spiritual man, the regenerated person, is one who has the Holy Spirit. This person is spiritually minded, thinks the thoughts of God (1 Corinthians 2:11-13), and lives by the Spirit of God (Romans 8:4-17). This individual believes in Jesus Christ, endeavors to follow the leading of the indwelling Spirit, resists sensual desires and is consistently putting to death the sinful deeds of the body (Romans 8:13-14).

Even though regenerated believers receive the new life of the Spirit, they retain the sinful nature with its evil inclinations (Galatians 5:16-21). The sinful nature that remains in them cannot be made good. It must be put to death and overcome through the power and grace of the Holy Spirit (Romans 8:13). They accomplish this by denying themselves daily (Titus 2:12), removing every hindrance of sin (Hebrews 12:1), and resisting all sinful inclinations (Galatians 5:16).

Believers, by the power of the Holy Spirit, must wage war against the sinful nature, crucify it, and put it to death daily. By this process of self-denial and yielding to the Holy Spirit's sanctifying work, believers in Christ will experience liberation from the power of their sinful nature and live their lives as Spiritual Christians (Romans 6:13).

Through the Holy Spirit, believers have insight into some of God's plans. Through the Holy Spirit, they can know God's thoughts, talk with Him, and expect answers to their prayers.

An intimate relationship with Christ comes only by spending time consistently in His presence. Your mind has to be renewed to the things of God in order to mature and become one with God.

> (3) The Carnal Christian is one who receives Christ into his life, or is born again, but does not do what is necessary to fully overcome the sinful nature. Paul notes in (1 Corinthians 3:1,3) that some of the Corinthian Christians were behaving in a carnal or fleshly way. Instead of consistently resisting the inclinations of their sinful nature, they yielded to some of them. They were not living in persistent disobedience, but they were compromising with the world, the flesh, and the devil in certain areas of their lives (2 Corinthians 6:14-18).

Carnality and rebellion were neither the total rule in their lives, nor had they entered into the serious immorality and unrighteousness that would separate them from the Kingdom of God (1 Corinthians 6:9-11). They were no longer growing in grace. Carnal Christians were behaving or acting as if they were not converts, and did not yet understand the full implication of salvation in Christ (1 Corinthians 3:1-2).

Their carnality was expressed in "envying, and strife," (1 Corinthians 3:3). They were indifferent to and tolerant of immorality within the Church. They did not take the Word of God or His Apostle with utmost seriousness (1 Corinthians 6:7-8).

The Carnal Christians of Corinth were in danger of being led astray from genuine and profound devotion to Christ, and being more and more conformed to the world (2 Corinthians 6:14-18).

Paul was afraid that when he came to Corinth, that God would humble him before the Corinthians who had sinned earlier and not repented. They had indulged in sexual sin, impurity, and debauchery. Some of these people excelled as leaders, and some possessed great gifts. Paul was afraid that the practices of wicked Corinth had invaded the congregation. He wrote sternly, hoping that they would straighten out their lives before he arrived.

We have to live differently than unbelievers, not allowing secular society to dictate how we are to treat others, or to attempt to set our standard of living. We cannot indulge in the same sins that the world indulges in. What harmony is there between Christ and Belial? What does a believer have in common with an unbeliever? What agreement is there between the temple of God and idols (2 Corinthians 6:15-16)?

Examine ourselves to see whether we are in the faith. Test ourselves. Do we not realize that Christ Jesus is in us—unless, of course, we fail the test (2 Corinthians 13:5)?

The Corinthians were called to examine and test themselves, to see if they were really Christians. Just as we get physical checkups, Paul also urges us to get spiritual checkups. We should look for a growing awareness of Christ's presence and power in our lives. Only then will we know if we are true Christians, or merely imposters. If we're not taking active steps to grow closer to God, we are drawing further away from Him.

The ultimate goal of every Christian is to follow the path of God, because this is the reason God created us. Our life, otherwise, will be in vain if we neglect to renew our mind to the things of God. The word of God says, "Seek first the Kingdom of God and His righteousness and all other things will be added unto us" (Matthew 6:33). The word seek means to attempt to find something, or an attempt or desire to obtain or achieve something. It is critical to seek God's Kingdom after salvation or being born again. Neglecting to seek His Kingdom will result in an unfulfilled life. God has a plan for each and every person on this Earth. In order to know the plan that He has for you, it is crucial to study His Word. Trust in Him with all of your heart, lean not to your own understanding, but in all your ways acknowledge Him and He will direct your path. (Proverbs 3:5-6). Amen!!!

DIFFERENT CLASSES OF PEOPLE REVIEW

1. The natural man cannot receive from _______________________________________.

2. Scripture normally divides humans into two classes: What are they?

   ____

   ____

3. What is the third class that we talked about? _______________________

   ____

   ____

4. The natural man is under the dominion of _______________________________.

5. Without the guidance of the _______________________________________,
   we cannot comprehend God.

6. The Spiritual man is the _______________________________________
   person. He has the Holy Spirit living inside him.

7. The Spiritual man lives by the _______________________________________.

8. An intimate relationship with Christ comes only by spending time consistently
   in His _______________________________________.

9. Is the carnal Christian born again?

Yes or No

10. What does he do differently from the Spiritual man?

____

____

____

____

____

11. It is critical to ____________________________________
  God's Kingdom after we are born again.

Chapter 6

HOW TO BECOME A SPIRITUAL MAN/WOMAN

When a person accepts by faith the salvation provided through Christ, he/she is regenerated. Regeneration is spiritual birth, or a re-creating and transformation of the person by God.

After the rebirth, the Holy Spirit comes to live inside us. As John 3:6 states, "Flesh gives birth to flesh, but the Spirit gives birth to spirit." Through this process, eternal life from God Himself is imparted to the believer. God loved us so much that He gave His only Son, that if we believe in Him we shall not perish but have eternal life. To all who received Him, to those who believed in His name, He gave the right to become children of God, children born neither of natural descent, nor of human decisions but born of God (John 1:12-13). Now a new person, you have taken off your old self with its practices and have put on the new self, which is being renewed in knowledge in the image of your Creator (Colossians 3:9-10).

Being renewed in knowledge means you have to be renewed, re-educated, and redirected to God's way of doing things. Romans 12:2 says, "Do not conform any longer to the pattern of this world, but be transformed by the renewing of your mind. Then you will be able to test and approve what God's will is–His good, pleasing and perfect will." God has a plan and purpose for each and every one of us. But, if we fail to accept Him, and renew our minds to His way of doing things, we will never discover what is our true purpose.

We have to honor and obey God. We must seek Him and His righteousness or His way of being and doing right. Unless we renew our minds, we will continue to walk in the same worldly behavior as we did previously. We have not been truly transformed. This is not a one-time thing. This is a continuous process throughout this life, until Jesus returns.

The new birth cannot be equated to physical birth, for the relationship of God with the believer is a matter of Spirit, rather than flesh. Regeneration involves a transition from an old life of sin to a new life of obedience to Jesus Christ.

CHOICES: "LIFE OR DEATH"

When Adam and Eve sinned, by eating the fruit from the tree of the knowledge of good and evil, moral and Spiritual death came immediately. However, physical death came later. Moral death meant the death of God's life in them, and their nature became sinful. Spiritual death meant their former relationship with God was destroyed.

Since the sin of Adam and Eve, every person is born into the world with a sinful nature. This sinful nature involves the innate desire to go our own selfish way, without concern for God or others. This nature was passed on to all human beings, but Jesus came, died, and was resurrected so that we would no longer have to live that sinful life. We have a choice to continue to live in sin or live the "born-again," abundant life of Christ.

> "This day I call heaven and earth as witnesses against you and I have set before you life and death, blessings, and curses. Now choose life, so that you and your children may live and that you may love the Lord your God, listen to His voice and hold fast to Him. For the Lord is your life, and will give you many years in the land he swore to give to your fathers, Abraham, Isaac, and Jacob" (Deuteronomy 30:19-20).

Here Moses is challenging Israel to choose life, to obey God and continue to experience His blessings. God does not force His will on anyone.

He let us make the decision to follow Him or to reject Him. This decision, however, is a life-or-death matter. God wants us to choose life, but this decision is totally up to us.

God's love for us is so great that He allows us to make our own choices. You may ask the question, "If He loves us so much, why would He let us go to hell?" Has anyone ever asked you to do something against your will? What do you do? Of course, you rebel and do not cooperate with the request. Well, this is why God will not do anything against your will. He wants you to love Him because that's your desire, and not because you are coerced or forced to love Him. He clearly tells us in Deuteronomy 30:19 to choose life. Choosing life means choosing God, because He is life.

Life is to live "after the Spirit," to seek and submit to the Holy Spirit's direction and enablement, and to concentrate our attention on the things of God. It means we live consciously at all times in the presence of God, trusting Him to give us the help and grace we need to accomplish His will in and through us.

Death is to live after the flesh (the sinful element of human nature). It is to desire, take pleasure in, be occupied with, and gratify the corrupt desires of sinful human nature. This sinful living includes not only fornication, adultery, hatred, selfish ambition, outburst of anger, but a total of 613 sins.

It is impossible to follow the flesh and the Spirit at the same time. Those who make the things of God their chief love and concern can expect eternal life and communion with God (Romans 8:10-11, 15-16).

What choice will you make? Will you choose Death or Life? Will we "Face Our Fears and Release Our Faith" to do God's will? The choice is ours!!!!!!!

HOW TO BECOME A
SPIRITUAL MAN/WOMAN REVIEW

1. **When a person accepts by Faith the Salvation provided through Christ, he is**

____

2. **When we are regenerated the** ________________________________
    comes to live in us.

3. **Is it true that each and every one of us on earth has a purpose?**

    Yes or No

4. **Is your mind instantly renewed when you become born again?**

    Yes or No

5. **When Adam and Eve committed the sin in the garden of Eden they died physically.**

    True or False

6. **When we are born into this world by our parents, we are born with a**
    ____ **nature.**

7. **What does God tell us to choose in Deuteronomy 30:19?**

    Life or Death

8. **Will He make the choice of life or death for you?**

Yes or No

9. **Choosing life means choosing God, because God is __________________________.**

10. **To live after the flesh is ____.**

11. **How many sins of the flesh are there? _________________________________.**

Chapter 7

QUESTIONS & ANSWERS SECTION
(Selah) Think About That

—⟨⟩—

Q. Why do we as Christians fall prey to the enemy? (Those that are mature and those that are immature). Have we become complacent or self-satisfied that we do not feel the need to please God?

A. **"Am I now trying to win the approval of men, or of God? Or am I trying to please men? If I were still trying to please men, I would not be a servant of Christ" (Galatians 1:10). We should, (as believers of the Gospel), make it our aim to please God even if it means displeasing some people. We were made for God's pleasure, and not for our own self-satisfaction or the satisfaction of others.**

Q. Why do we, as Christians, sometimes allow the flesh to overcome us?

A. **We are human, and after we are born again, we must renew our minds. This is a process. It does not happen instantly. We still have residue from the old man and the more we renew our minds, the more likely we are to be able to conquer the flesh. We will be continuing to perfect ourselves until Jesus returns. This is why Jesus died for us, so we would not have to pay the penalty for sin.**

Because there is no good thing in the flesh, the enemy will try to overcome you with the pressures and cares of life. When the enemy comes in, the Spirit of the Lord will lift up a standard against him (which is the Word of God). This will destroy any plans that he has schemed against you.

Q. Why is it so important to be Disciples? The Disciplined ones? Living Epistles?

A. We are living examples of Jesus. We are a representation of the Holy One, set aside for God's use only. God made us for His glory. We have the love of God in our hearts that is shed abroad by the precious Holy Spirit. As we are true disciples, this love can be perceived by the natural man, allowing him the opportunity to make a wise choice to give his life to Jesus and become a spiritual man. If we, being spiritual men, neglect to discipline ourselves, what example will the world have to follow? Jesus left this job for us to do. This is our purpose for being here on earth. Let us not neglect our call to do the will of God.

Q. Who are we listening to?

A. Be careful who you allow to commune or fellowship with you. Do not be unequally yoked with unbelievers—do not make mismatched alliances with them, or come under a different yoke with them (inconsistent with your faith). What has a believer in common with an unbeliever? What agreement can there be between a temple of God and idols? The unbeliever is going to try to get you to see what he sees. If he has no knowledge of God, he is blinded to the truth.

> This does not mean that you cannot befriend unbelievers (or how else would we win them), but we cannot allow them to influence us, to engage in their sinful lifestyles. We must stay on guard against the flattery and smooth speech that will lead us into sin, whereas, they end up changing our mindset into the way they are thinking.

> The sins of the flesh are the devil's playground, and he usually win on his turf. Don't play on his playground. Keep him in your territory. Be subjected to God. Stand firm against the devil. Resist him and he will flee from you (James 4:7).

Q. Does the Word come to condemn?

A. Of course not, it comes to make us free. "Therefore, there is no condemnation—no adjudging guilty of wrong—for those who are in Christ Jesus, who live not after the dictates of the flesh, but after the dictates of the Spirit. For the law of the Spirit of Life (which is) in Christ Jesus (the law of our new being), has freed us from the law of sin and death" (Romans 8:1-2 Amp).

Do not be a slave to sin because that is the worst type of slavery. If we deliberately live in sin, because we refuse to believe that the word is true, we are slaves to sin. The wages of sin are death. God has made us free from slavery to sin. God has given us freedom to live our lives more abundantly. "Thank God for His freedom through His Son Jesus the Christ."

AMEN!!!!!!!

CONCLUSION

It is truly my heart's desire that after reading the book (Facing Our Fears, Releasing Our Faith) and studying the work-book, you will be able to better understand the message. These books are only an introduction to the Kingdom of God.

As stated at the beginning of this workbook, I pray that these lessons on the Kingdom of Satan and the Kingdom of God will bring more clarity, and shed more light into the lives of people who are presently walking in darkness. I thank God that those who confess Jesus as Lord and Savior will be better able (by the Holy Spirit) to separate the darkness from the light and to be able to know the difference.

I pray that these lessons have given the unsaved something to think about (Selah) and consider becoming saved. If you have never asked Christ to come into your life, now is the time. This is the most important step that you will ever take. Say, "Jesus, I confess that I am a sinner. I believe that you are the Son of God and that you died on the cross to save me from my sins. Forgive me Lord of all my sins and cleanse my heart from all unrighteousness. I thank you for saving me, in Jesus name, Amen."

If you have spoken this prayer from your heart, you are ready to begin a new life in Christ, or in the Spirit. The Holy Spirit will lead and guide you into all truths.

Salvation is the first step. After you receive Jesus as your personal savior, seek Him and His way of doing things. You have to seek in order to renew your mind to the things of God. This is inevitable. If you don't seek Him, you will not understand what or why you have to live for Him. It is a process. All these things will not happen overnight, but the more you seek the more He reveals Himself to you and you will desire to be like Him.

" But first and most importantly seek (aim at, strive after) His Kingdom and His righteousness (His way of doing and being right-the attitude and character of God), and all these things will be given to you also" (Matthew 6:33 Amp).

ANSWER KEY:

THE TWO KINGDOMS REVIEW:

1. (1) The Kingdom of God
    (2) The Kingdom of Satan
2. God
3. Satan
4. God
5. Jesus
6. Theocracy
7. Faith
8. System of belief
9. (1) Principalities, (2) Powers, (3) Rulers of Darkness, (4) Spirit wickedness in high places
10. False
11. Fear
12. Enemy
13. Sinful nature
14. True
15. Be born again
16. Renew your mind
17. We will be in error
    We will not know what is right, from what is wrong
    We will continue to live the same way we did before being saved
18. Studying the word of God

Chapter 1
THE KINGDOM OF DARKNESS: (SATAN'S KINGDOM) REVIEW:

1. Sinful or selfish
2. Satan
3. (1) He is evil (2) He is a lier (3) He is a thief (4) He is a murderer
4. True

5. A highly systemized army or empire of evil spirit forces with rank and order.
6. By Christ dying on the cross
7. Redeemed
8. A mindset, a way of thinking
9. (1) Fornication (2) Hatred (3) Wrath (4) Reveling
10. 613

Chapter 2:
DESCRIPTION OF THE WORKS OF THE FLESH FORNICATION REVIEW:

1. Voluntary sexual intercourse between two unmarried persons or two persons who are not married to each other.
2. Word
3. Lord
4. Body
5. Holy Spirit
6. Christ
7. Christ's control
8. (1) Procreation (2) pleasure (3) husband (4) wife
9. Christ
10. Sin
11. Escape
12. Holy Spirit
13. (1) Free (2) bondage
14. Renew
15. One
16. Sin
17. Self-gratification
18. (1) Unwanted pregnancy
    (2) Contract an STD
    (3) You sin against your own body
19. False

IDOLATRY REVIEW:

1. The worship of a physical object as a God. Immoderate attachment or devotion to something.
2. (1) Material (2) physical
3. Idols
4. Covetousness
5. It distorts the truth and leads people away from God.

6. Flee
7. (1) Money (2) Fame (3) Material things
8. Love
9. God
10. Word
11. Spiritually
12. Faith
13. (1) It displeases God (2) It reduces God in our lives.
14. Abundantly

HATRED REVIEW:

1. Intense hostility, and aversion usually deriving from fear, anger, or sense of injury. Extreme dislike or disgust.
2. Emotion
3. Rejects
4. (1) Love (2) Compassion (3) Holiness
5. (1) Evil doers (2) injustice
6. True
7. Violence
8. Haman
9. Love
10. Heart
11. (1) Hatred pollutes your spirit
12. If you don't like a person, limit your contact

ADULTERY REVIEW:

1. (1) Voluntary (2) married
2. Transgress
3. Sin
4. Divorce
5. True
6. False
7. (1) Guilt and shame (2) loss of trust and intimacy

STRIFE REVIEW:

1. Vigorous or bitter conflict, discord, antagonism; A quarrel, struggle, or clash.
2. Devil

3. Envy
4. Demons
5. Humility
6. Pride
7. God
8. (1) Love (2) Freedom
9. The thief comes only to steal and kill and destroy; I have come that they may have life, and have it more abundantly.
10. (1) Strife brings conflict, spread anger and confusion
11. (1) By walking in love and unity (2) Refuse to hold grudges
    (3) forgive.

LASCIVIOUSNESS REVIEW:

1. Inclined to lustfulness; Inciting sexual desires. Expressing lust or lewdness. Arousing or inciting sexual desire.
2. Sensuality
3. (1) Men who lay with men (2) Women who lay with women
4. Having ceased to care
5. Our conduct
6. False
7. False
8. Renew
9. True
10. Bible
11. Bondage
12. Imprisonment; One could contract a disease.

WRATH (Anger) REVIEW:

1. The feeling of strong displeasure turned against anyone or anything that has hurt or wronged us or others. Explosive anger or rage which flares into violent words or deeds.
2. No
3. Word of God
4. Anger
5. Sin
6. Divide
7. Ferocious
8. Rage
9. (1) Hypertension (2) Depression

10. Love
11. Forgiveness
12. False
13. (1) Loss of employment (2) Incarceration

VARIANCE REVIEW:

1. Being variable, divergent, different, or deviate; disagreement
2. Personalities
3. God
4. False
5. God
6. All
7. True
8. (1) Family separations (2) Stress disorders (3) Hostile work environments

EMULATIONS REVIEW:

1. An effort or desire to equal or excel others; Jealous rivalry; Competition.
2. No
3. The love of God
4. (1) This Spirit will lead you into a snare and cause an angry spirit with all kinds of evil.
   (2) You will never grow past your insecurities if you always try to compete with others.
BONUS: Personal answer

DRUNKENNESS REVIEW:

1. Habitual or excessive drinking of intoxicants. The condition of being drunk.
2. Alcohol
3. He will begin to sweat, become nauseated, have withdrawal Symptoms, anxiety, and shaking.
4. Drug
5. To cope with problems such as peer pressure.
6. False
7. True
8. 88,000 (62,000 Men & 26,000 Women)
9. True
10. (1) Short attention span (2) Impaired judgment (3) Loss of Memory (4) Delayed motor reactions (5) Incarceration

ENVYING (Jealousy) REVIEW:

1. A sense of discontent or jealousy with regard to another's advantage, successions, and possessions, etc. Desire for an advantage possessed by another.
2. Devil
3. Possess you
4. False
5. Forever
6. True
7. True
8. False
9. (1) Being jealous will cause bitterness (2) Being jealous will bring hopelessness and depression.

HERESY REVIEW:

1. Religious doctrines or opinions rejected by the authorities of a church, as contrary to the established beliefs of that church. The maintenance of such an opinion or doctrine.
2. False
3. True
4. True
5. Christ
6. Gospel
7. Yes
8. Yes
9. (1) It causes confusion for unbelievers. (2) Heresy brings trouble to the church; those who embrace it are put into condemnation.

REVELING REVIEW:

1. To make merry. To take great pleasure or delight. To indulge in boisterous festivities. Boisterous merrymaking or festivity.
2. Sin
3. False
4. Because of wickedness
5. Satan
6. (1) We may turn to unhealthy relationships. (2) We may indulge in wild parties and Substance abuse.
7. Destroyed
8. If you are a Christian, act like one. Allow the Holy Spirit to lead you.
9. Overindulgence can lead to incarceration. You could harm yourself or someone else.

SEDITIONS REVIEW:

1. An incitement of public disorder or rebellion against authority. Rebellious disorder.
2. True
3. True
4. Wickedness
5. Word
6. (1) Ruinous or destructive (2) helpful
7. Arguments or quarrels
8. Raising objections over trivial matters can cause strife and division.

MURDER REVIEW:

1. The killing of another human being, in contrast to accidental homicide or causing the death of another person in war or in defense of one's property.
2. (1) Love (2) Anger
3. Anger
4. Death
5. Murderer
6. His jealous anger
7. False
8. Bitterness
9. Bitterness
10. (1) Kill (2) Steal (3) Destroy
11. False
12. God
13. Capital Punishment

WITCHCRAFT REVIEW:

1. The art or practices of a witch; sorcery, magic. Magical influence, Witchery.
2. Witch
3. Evil
4. God
5. (1) Satan (2) demons
6. (1) The Bible (2) His, Son, Jesus (3) The Holy Spirit
7. True
8. The denial of the essential doctrines of the Christian Faith
9. Take your eyes off God and focus on the leader of the cult.
10. (1) The spirit of witchcraft is deceptive. The witchcraft spirit will cause one to walk in error.

Chapter 3:
RELEASING OUR FAITH REVIEW:

1. God
2. (1) Glory (2) honor
3. (1) Purpose (2) goals
4. No
5. (1) God is Love (2) God is a Spirit (3) God is creator (4) God is wise (5) God is eternal (6) He is trustworthy.
6. God
7. (1) Love (2) Peace (3) Joy (4) Long-suffering (5) Gentleness (6) Meekness (7) Goodness (8) Temperance (9) Faith
8. No
9. The Holy Spirit
10. Yes
11. The Holy Spirit

Chapter 4:
DESCRIPTION OF THE FRUIT OF THE SPIRIT LOVE REVIEW:

1. Love is the benevolent affection of God for His creatures or the reverent affection due from them to God.
2. (1) Love suffers long (2) Love is kind (3) Love is not puffed up (4) Love is not easily provoked.
3. False
4. Charity or Love
5. False
6. (1) Build-up, (2) serve (3) strengthen
7. Love
8. Love
9. (1) Faith (2) Love
10. Christ
11. God
12. Yes
13. Choice or decision
14. (1) Patience (2) stability
15. No

PEACE REVIEW:

1. Wholeness, unity, harmony, prosperity, health, and fulfillment. Shalom, well-being, soundness.
2. Satan
3. Destroy
4. True
5. The Holy Spirit
6. No
7. Personal Answer

JOY REVIEW:

1. An inner sense of exultation and confidence in God which the Holy Spirit works in the lives of believers, and which we experience despite present sufferings.
2. Salvation
3. God
4. Happiness
5. True joy
6. Jesus Christ
7. Perseverance
8. Yes
9. God's
10. Joy
11. God

LONGSUFFERING (Patience) REVIEW:

1. Patience
2. Perish
3. False
4. Day
5. Scoffers
6. Yes
7. Self-controlled
8. Patience
9. In the Garden of Eden when Adam and Eve sinned.
10. True
11. False

GENTLENESS REVIEW:

1. (1) Kind (2) amiable
2. False
3. Angry
4. True
5. Spirit
6. Peace
7. Gentle
8. Holy Spirit
9. (1) Quarrels (2) Foolish arguments

MEEKNESS REVIEW:

1. The quality or state of being meek; A mild, moderate, humble, or submissive quality.
2. 'Anawah
3. Arrogance
4. Faith
5. Humble
6. False
7. Yourselves
8. True
9. Humble
10. Pride
11. Jesus humbled Himself as a man and was obedient to death on the cross, so we could have eternal life.

GOODNESS REVIEW:

1. The state or quality of being good. Moral excellence, Virtue, Kindness, Generosity.
2. God
3. True
4. God
5. Trust
6. Ephesus
7. Security
8. God
9. Workmanship

FAITH REVIEW:

1. Confidence or trust in a person or thing. Belief in God. Obligation or loyalty or fidelity to a person, promise, engagement, etc.
2. Now Faith is the substance of things hoped for, the evidence of things not seen.
3. Faith
4. Righteousness
5. Faith
6. Yes
7. True
8. True
9. Hearing
10. Word

TEMPERANCE–(Self-control) REVIEW:

1. Power over one's own actions; Moderation; Good sense.
2. Temper
3. Control
4. Self-control
5. False
6. (1) Defense (2) Protection
7. Holy Spirit
8. Devil
9. Christ

COMMENTS ON FRUIT OF THE SPIRIT REVIEW:

1. No
2. True
3. No
4. Holy Spirit
5. True
6. (1) The sinful nature (flesh) (2) The Holy Spirit
7. Holy Spirit
8. True

Chapter 5
DIFFERENT CLASSES OF PEOPLE REVIEW:

1. God
2. (1) The Natural man (2) Spiritual man
3. The Carnal Christian
4. Satan
5. Holy Spirit
6. Regenerated
7. Spirit of God
8. Presence
9. Yes
10. He does not study the Word of God or renew his mind.
11. Seek

Chapter 6:
HOW TO BECOME A SPIRITUAL MAN/WOMAN REVIEW

1. Regenerated
2. Holy Spirit
3. Yes
4. No
5. False
6. Sinful
7. Life
8. No
9. Life
10. Death
11. 613

REFERENCES

Unless otherwise indicated, all scripture quotations in this workbook are from the King James Version of the Bible.

CHAPTER 1

1. Page 15; Fornication, The Random House Dictionary
2. Page 21; Article by Brian C. Thomas at www.god1st.org, Consequences of Sex Before Marriage
3. Page 25; Idolatry, Merriam Webster since 1828
4. Page 29; 2Cherish2Commend.com
5. Page 32; Hatred, Merriam Webster since 1828
6. Page 35-36; Consequences of hatred, www.everydayhealth.com
7. Page 39; Adultery, Merriam Webster since 1828
8. Page 42; Consequences of Adultery by Lesli White at www.beliefnet.com
9. Page 45; Strife, The Random House Dictionary
10. Page 49; Consequences of Strife by Creflo Dollar, Creflodollarministries.org
11. Page 52; Lasciviousness, The Random House Dictionary
12. Page 55; Legal dictionary.net
13. Page 58; Wrath, The Scott Foresman Advanced Dictionary
14. Page 64; Variance, The Random House Dictionary
15. Page 68; Emulations, The Random House Dictionary
16. Page 74; Drunkenness, Merriam Webster Dictionary
17. Page 75; Statistics on Alcoholism from www.niaaa.nih.gov
18. Page 77-78; Consequences of Alcoholism at Americanaddictioncenters.org
19. Page 81; Envyings, The Random House Dictionary
20. Page 84; Consequences of Envy or Jealousy, Ncrealities.wordpress.com
21. Page 86; Heresies, The Random House Dictionary
22. Page 91; Consequences of Heresy at Against-heresies.blogspot.com
23. Page 95; Reveling, The Random House Dictionary
24. Page 102; Seditions, The Random House Dictionary
25. Page 107; Murders, The Revell Bible Dictionary
26. Page 113; Witchcraft, The Random House Dictionary

27. Page 116; Article at <u>www.allaboutcults.org</u>.

28. Page 130; Love, The Random House Dictionary

29. Page 138; Peace, The Revell Bible Dictionary

30. Page 144; Joy, The Revell Bible Dictionary

31. Page 156; Gentleness, The Random House Dictionary

32. Page 159; Meekness, Merriam Webster Dictionary since 1828

33. Page 164; Goodness, The Random House Dictionary

34. Page 168; Faith, The Random House Dictionary

35. Page 173; Temperance, The Revell Bible Dictionary

Lightning Source UK Ltd.
Milton Keynes UK
UKHW030241131120
373269UK00008B/216